I0934249

CARROLL COUNTY
COMMUNITY COLLEGE CENTER
WITHDRAWN

NOV. 1983

Crosscurrents / MODERN CRITIQUES

Harry T. Moore, *General Editor*

ARNOLD J. TOYNBEE
Historian for
an Age
in Crisis

Roland N. Stromberg

WITH A PREFACE BY

Harry T. Moore

SOUTHERN ILLINOIS UNIVERSITY PRESS
Carbondale and Edwardsville

FEFFER & SIMONS, INC.
London and Amsterdam

Copyright © 1972 by Southern Illinois University Press
All rights reserved
Printed in the United States of America
Designed by Andor Braun
International Standard Book Number 0–8093–0546–1
Library of Congress Catalog Card Number 74–180629

Contents

Preface

The Crosscurrents/Modern Critiques series recently celebrated the publication of its hundredth volume, and still other items are scheduled to appear. These books (one of them an anthology of contemporary American poetry) have dealt entirely with literature. And now we present a study of the most notable historian of our time, Arnold J. Toynbee. But why have a historian in this series?

There are many reasons. For one, Roland N. Stromberg wrote it. He is the author of several excellent books on world history and of the outstanding volume, An Intellectual History of Western Europe. First published in 1966, it is now going into a new edition. Besides covering the subject in general, it is often valuable in its discussions of literature, which takes on a new perspective when viewed in the context of intellectual history. The section on Romanticism places that topic in the center of events of its time, and it is particularly interesting when seen in terms of its milieu. The same may be said of one of the subdivisions of the chapter "The West in Trouble: From World War I to World War II," with its admirable comments on "Literature and Thought Between the Wars," which deal not only with such manifestations as surrealism and dadaism, but also with the leading authors of the time. Professor Stromberg (of the University of Wisconsin-Milwaukee) is extremely well equipped to discuss literature and other arts. (Interestingly, just as this volume is going to the printer, the Oxford University

Press is sponsoring, at the National Book League, London, an exhibition of manuscripts, proofs, and varying editions under the name of "A Study of Toynbee.")

A further reason for the appearance here of this book on Arnold J. Toynbee is that Toynbee writes literature as well as history. This doesn't mean merely that he writes poetry (in Greek!) or engages in various other forms of literature, but rather that, like Dr. Stromberg, he breaks down the barriers which so many people have set up between literature and history. It seems to me that it is quite safe to say, in the teeth of literary isolationism, that students of literature should be aware of history in all its phases, as well as drawing upon such subjects as psychology and philosophy. Toynbee is a particularly interesting figure to study, even if his work has been rather savagely attacked (a matter which Dr. Stromberg deals with) by some other historians; Toynbee presents, at more than one level, a formidable challenge.

This book is, then, for students of literature as well as for students of history. It is the first of its kind, offering a many-sided view of Arnold Toynbee. We hope that it will send students of history and literature—and other readers from other disciplines—to Toynbee's own books.

The present volume, however, is more than a mere "guide"; it is in the fullest sense a critique. It is of course an introduction to Toynbee's work, but it also presents an evaluation. It is especially interesting in its summary of the criticisms and its response to them.

The chapter dealing with the criticism follows a neatly compressed survey of Toynbee's life, works, and career. As for the criticism, Toynbee himself answered much of it in the twelfth and final volume of A Study of History. Toynbee corrected minor errors by tipped-in errata sheets in the later volumes of his work, according to Professor Stromberg, who notes further, "The magnitude of his subject makes errors of this sort inevitable." Various commentators, both pro- and anti-Toynbee, have regretted that he even bothered to answer his detractors. One kind of criticism is typified by Professor Hans Kohn, who declared that historians, even while disagreeing with the author of A Study of History, "will be indebted to Dr. Toynbee for a provocative inspiration to think again, and to think out of a deeper knowledge." It is a rarity that a book devoted to a single author incorporates so much criticism of his work, as well as a set of reasonable and good-natured comments on these critiques.

The following and final chapter, "Toynbee's Mind and Art," is of course the crux of this volume. It deals further with the adverse criticism, but makes plain the essential value of Toynbee, no matter how many big or little faults may be found in his work. To some readers, he is too religious, to others he is insufficiently Marxist, and so on. Whatever stance one may take, often conditioned by one's temperament in the area of ideals, Toynbee is a great adventure in reading, as every line of Professor Stromberg's valuable study makes clear. It is a pleasure to welcome this book into the Crosscurrents/Modern Critiques series, for it is an extremely valuable contribution to a subject that should engage historians, literary men, and even those who work in other disciplines. The book is, in any event, valuable, in terms of Toynbee's title, for a study of history—and as all of Dr. Stromberg's own works have indicated, history is not a separate entity: it has a vital relation to literature also, and it should be known to many others, if only as an understanding of the elements of our thinking and feeling.

HARRY T. MOORE

Southern Illinois University
March 21, 1972

Introduction

Arnold J. Toynbee is now (1972) eighty-three years old, and still showing remarkable vigor, but no one will question that his claim to immortality rests on the monumental *A Study of History*, substantially published between 1934 and 1954. He has given us many other volumes on world affairs, on his travels, on religious and moral problems, and enough other subjects to qualify him as one of the most prolific writers since H. G. Wells. Unlike Wells he has never turned his pen to fiction, unless we adopt the view of some of his critics that his historical system amounts to no more than that. (He has written a little poetry, mostly in Greek, which he modestly proffers to us at the end of his auto-biographical *Experiences*, published in 1969.) In his later years he has become something of a public prophet much in demand on the lecture circuit and in popular magazines; it is unlikely that posterity will read this output except as an aid to understanding the author of *A Study of History*.

Of the genius of the latter there cannot, really, be any doubt. Its reputation has sharply declined in some circles. "Ten years ago," a well-known scholar wrote a few years ago, "Arnold J. Toynbee bestrode the earth like a colossus. . . . Today, the Toynbee tide seems to have run its course." [1] The 1940s were filled with cries of amazement at what one reviewer, himself a distinguished historian, described as "a range of knowledge and subtlety of insight which leave the reader breathless." [2] It is true that criticism was never absent. Writing as early as 1939, when the second set of three volumes was published (unquestionably the most impressive of the series), Leonard Woolf, while paying tribute to "a very remarkable book," observed that "the more one reads his book the more doubtful one becomes of the legitimacy of his general method and the soundness of his conclusions." [3] The doubt grew into a near certainty, and attacking Toynbee, who offered one of the broadest targets in history, became a widespread intellectual pastime in the 1950s. Whole volumes were published consisting of the collected reproaches, sneers, and refutations of the scholarly community. [4] With infinite patience and much apparent humility, but little real repentance, Toynbee dedicated the twelfth and last volume of his *Study* to answering his critics, and used up some 675 pages in so doing. [5]

After all this chorus, first of praise and then of rebuke, there may be little to say that is new, but it seems time for a summation. How are we to judge the war between Toynbee and his foes? What will be the great historian's final place in history? Will he vanish entirely, like some other savants much idolized by their contemporaries whom now nobody reads? Will he join Buckle and Marx and Spencer and Spengler in the ranks of the splendid failures, who essayed the impossible task of capturing the secret of man's social evolution, and will never be forgotten even though they could not succeed? He may take rank well above them, as assuredly his knowledge of history far exceeded theirs. It is possible that no one will again have the courage to launch upon the task Toynbee set himself, that his failure registers the decisive check to a certain kind of dream about total understanding of the past. But Toynbee is surely right in his claim that man needs and seeks this sort of understanding to guide him in a bewildering world. [6] And at least a few are not convinced that the quest for a true science of the past along Toynbeean lines must always fail, even though he did.[7] It is possible to detect a slight turn of the tide back toward Toynbee today, after the reaction of the '50s.

It is quite possible that, leaving aside irrelevant considerations of "complete success," which no one achieves, and accepting that all thinkers reflect their age, Toynbee will be remembered as the great historian of our times—of the era of twentieth-century world wars. As Gibbon, Macaulay, and Burckhardt spoke for their epochs, so Toynbee will represent ours to posterity, assuming there is a posterity. No other historian of this century rivals him in scope, in style, in theme, in sheer stature. His preoccupation with the decay of civilizations as much as his astonishing command of an incredible range of knowledge about all the civilizations of the world mark him as a figure of the twentieth century, wherein technical proficiency accompanies social breakdown. That he has intruded into his supposedly empirical and objective research so much religious vision does not make him less a candidate for immortality. Other historians may grumble, but this sort of vision, which Augustine, Voltaire, and Marx possessed, signals the historical imagination at its greatest. On the other hand, we will have to take into account the still widespread conviction that Toynbee is one of the greatest frauds of our fraudulent age, a man almost constitutionally incapable of getting his facts straight, incredibly arrogant in his claims to omniscience, a dabbler in the spurious and dangerous field of "meta-history" and not even a good metaphysician. It is a curious divergence of opinion, one which itself perhaps sheds light on our modern intellectual culture, so complex and divided against itself.

Now that he has completed his work, and a generation of criticism has been produced, it should be a propitious moment to attempt a balanced view of Toynbee and to arrive at a just estimate of his place in modern thought. The volume of commentary has grown so great that several years ago (even before Toynbee's

Reconsiderations) a prominent historian, introducing his own essay on Toynbee, remarked that "to add still one more comment on Mr. Toynbee's Study of History may well appear sheer effrontery." [8] This volume does not hope to say anything new about Toynbee, and only a far more extensive study could aspire to supply the "definitive" treatment of Toynbee. My aim is a modest one: to present him to new readers and to offer an interim report on him as historian, social theorist, and contemporary writer. The fact is that while essays are numerous full treatments of Toynbee are scarce. Part prophet in spite of his disclaimers, in his way part poet, commentator on his times, Toynbee is a major contemporary figure. He is a man of his times, for even the historian, who tries to step outside time and look at man *sub specie aeternitatis*, remains himself a product of his era, and is subsumed by the processes he is trying to understand—caught in its crosscurrents.

ROLAND N. STROMBERG

University of Wisconsin—Milwaukee
December 1971

Arnold J. Toynbee

If men could learn from history, what lessons it might teach us!
—COLERIDGE

1

Career and Writings

Toynbee's Early Career

Lord Acton's advice to "look behind history at the "historian" is doubtless valuable; but our concern in this short book is primarily with the work and not the man (*ad hominem*, as Toynbee would say), and the time is hardly yet ripe for a full-scale Toynbee biography. His own works—here and there in *A Study of History*, especially volumes 10 and 12, as well as in his *Acquaintances* and *Experiences* (1967, 1969)—throw a good deal of light on a rich, late-Victorian and Edwardian early life, climaxed by perhaps the best education the world could offer (Winchester, Oxford), even if "old-fashioned"; and on a busy and successful career in the still closely knit, marvelously stimulating world of British political *cum* intellectual society, a world where one consorted as a matter of course with such men as James Bryce, Lewis Namier, Gilbert Murray, and was not too far from the corridors of power where Lloyd George and Churchill walked. Toynbee's life seems to have been a serene and happy one, in contrast to the foreboding gloom, as it is often construed, of his historical masterpiece. This life was of course broken across by the tragedies of history; and as he does not allow us to forget, Toynbee was of that generation which experienced the incredible shock of World War I. But by natural temperament he seems to belong not with those writers who revolt against their environment and set out on a quest for new values, but rather with those who seek consciously to perpetuate a cherished tradition, and with all piety "be as their fathers were." In *Reconsiderations*, Annex 2, Toynbee discusses the charge that he has been alienated from his culture, a charge made because of his crusade against nationalistic history and Western-oriented history. He recalls his rebellion against excessive doses of English history, and finds Western man guilty of many sins and much arrogance. But he defends his education, and his immersion in what his friend Sir Ernest Barker called the Western "traditions of civility" is an obvious and ubiquitous feature of his whole style and personality.

Though Toynbee made his way to the educational top via the familiar route of examinations, he was co-opted into the elite from well down in the social scale; the family was not a wealthy one. It might even be possible to detect something of the arriviste's anxiety in the furious energy which has driven Toynbee to write and write and write (and, in a curiously petty-bourgeois way, to publish everything, wasting no single line however repetitious or trivial—as anyone who has read all of Toynbee will understand all too well). There is in him a little of H. G. Wells and Herbert Spencer, those classic British lower middle-class outsiders and haters of the Oxbridge intellectual establishment; for while paying grateful tribute to this classical education he has consistently noted its drawbacks in not acquainting him with the "practical" world," he has admired Americanism and energy, and has sought to get in touch with the contemporary world by diligent traveling. "Oxford above and Manchester below"—perhaps the famous description of Gladstone helps, *mutatis mutandis*, to define Toynbee. He did, after all, in a decision he has described as one of the most critical in his life, choose to leave his post as an Oxford don, eventually to take up another career with the Royal Institute of International Affairs.

Nevertheless his family heritage was, intellectually and spiritually, a distinguished one. Its outstanding characteristics were a love of scholarship, humanitarianism, and a deep Christian piety (Anglican, "latitudinarian"). In a striking degree the author of A *Study of History* reproduced these characteristics. The influence of family background and a family tradition appear as unusually strong forces in the shaping of his mind and personality. His grandfather, Joseph Toynbee, was a distinguished surgeon, famous as a pioneer in aural surgery, but hardly less renowned as a philanthropist who was tireless in his efforts to improve workingmen's conditions of life during the ugly early days of England's industrial revolution—altogether a remarkable personality. He left a numerous progeny, and several of his sons were to have notable careers. A. J. Toynbee's father was a social worker; one of his uncles (Paget Toynbee) was a distinguished philologist and Dante scholar (d. 1932); another uncle, the most famous, was the brilliant Arnold Toynbee (author of the still read *Lectures on the Industrial Revolution*) who died in 1883 after having made for himself, in a brief life of less than thirty-one years, a reputation as scholar, philanthropist, social philosopher, and exceptional personality.[1] There are some rather striking similarities between the first and the second Arnold Toynbees. The uncle, like the nephew, was passionately interested in history; he was deeply religious yet a searching scholar, a child of the Enlightenment who believed that Christianity, whose truths were symbolic and indestructible, would be strengthened rather than weakened by historical criticism; he continued the family interest in reform and humanitarianism, being concerned above all else with ameliorating the workers' conditions of life and checking the ravages of an industrialism destructive of human life. One who has read and studied both men will be struck by these and other, more subtle, similarities.[2]

Toynbee's mother was notable for having been one

of the first women to receive a degree from an English university; and to her he has paid tribute as the one "who first turned his thoughts towards History as being a historian herself." [3] Among other influences, Toynbee mentioned an indebtedness to his early reading of Freeman's *Historical Essays*.[4] In sum, he grew up in a family circle rich with traditions of scholarship, love of literature, Christian piety, humanitarianism, and quest for philosophic truth—a family not unusually wealthy (Toynbee has called it "by Late-Victorian British middle-class standards poor") but with entrée via the public schools and university into England's intellectual elite; altogether a rare and splendid family background, and one which had given promise of producing scholars of unusual quality.

Arnold J. Toynbee followed in his uncle's footsteps by becoming a fellow and tutor of Balliol College, Oxford, at the age of twenty-three; this was in 1912. His field was ancient history. He had received, at Winchester and Oxford, an old-fashioned education in Greek and Latin classics, following which "I spent nine months [November 1911 to August 1912] travelling on foot through the old territories of Greece as well as in Krete and the Athos peninsula . . . ," studying the historical geography of the country and social and economic conditions as well.[5] During the 1911–12 year, too, he studied archaeology and classics at Athens. In *Acquaintances* and *Experiences*, his recent volumes of reminiscences, Toynbee has fondly recollected treasured memories of this *Wanderjahr*. Did he, here in Greece, pondering the great ruins, like Gibbon in Rome, first conceive his project of a comparative study of the decay of civilizations? Perhaps; but a far more potent stimulus to the young historian's thoughts was the shocking outbreak of war in 1914. In his first book, published in 1915, *Nationality and the War*, he wrote,

> If inspiration fails them in this hour, then we are witnessing "the beginning of great evils for Hellas"

and the Sovereign Nations of Europe are doomed to the same destruction as the Sovereign Cities of Greece. (P. 500)

He has testified that the war of 1914 made Thucydides, which he was teaching to college students, suddenly seem meaningful and contemporary.[6] The war stimulated him to his first important historical writings, and it worked powerfully on his mind and imagination, as it did on all sensitive men; it focused his thought squarely on the problem of his civilization and its "time of troubles." He had returned to his post at Oxford and shown promise of extraordinary abilities. In 1913 he married Rosalind Murray, daughter of the renowned classical scholar Gilbert Murray. In 1913 he published an article on Sparta in a learned journal, which a present-day scholar has described as typically Toynbeean in its boldness of hypothesis; perhaps but for the war he would have settled into an academic groove and become another Gilbert Murray or a Rostovtzeff. But the outbreak of war drew him into the government service.

He worked during the war for the Political Intelligence Department of the Foreign Office, chiefly on Turkish affairs. He edited the Blue Book published in 1916 by the British government on the *Treatment of Americans in the Ottoman Empire*. He made himself, too, an authority on German atrocities in Europe, and wrote several pamphlets in which, using available sources such as eye-witness accounts and official documents, he presented the case against German occupation policy in Belgium, France, and Poland.[7] The extent to which Toynbee allowed himself to be drawn into propaganda activities at the expense of historical truth is a question we will not attempt to decide here. Older and better men than the young scholar was at that time did the same thing. It may only be observed that his distinguished mentor, Lord James Bryce, appeared to many later historians as the epitome of guillibility if not downright mendacity in his reports on German atrocities, but

Sir Llewellyn Woodward says these have been substantially confirmed.[8] Toynbee clearly was later somewhat ashamed of this episode. He remained convinced
that Germany in World War I was the unmitigated
"aggressor" (at least he says that at one point in *A
Study of History*), but he also talks critically about the
hatreds unleashed and the power of the press lords. In
Experiences (pp. 304–5), he refers to his "noxious war
work" and compares it to his Uncle Percy Frankland's
work on poison gas: "we behaved irresponsibly." There
is no doubt about Toynbee's regrets over his war-propa-
ganda activity. (Nevertheless, on p. 207 he indicates
his belief that there *were* German atrocities in Belgium
and France.)

Toynbee has described (*A Study of History*, 10,
236–37 and *Experiences*, p. 38) how he was kept from
military service by the accident of the dysentery he
acquired from drinking contaminated water while
tramping through Greece in 1912. One may conjecture
that this intensified his urge to render patriotic service
with his pen—as indeed, it seems to have impelled him
to write all his life, for he had been spared to do creative
labor while so many of his friends and fellow students
were killed in that assassination of a generation. Of
the Armenian atrocities, which he personally observed,
he says simply that they taught him Original Sin: he
saw quite enough of the war's evil here.

But his most important wartime works were two books
in which he endeavored to do some constructive historical thinking about the problem of Europe and of Western civilization, both appearing in 1915: *Nationality
and the War* and *The New Europe*. The former was a
careful study in historical and political geography, trying
to work out what national feeling is, by what means it
can be satisfied, and how Europe might be recon-
structed on the basis of nationality. *The New Europe*,
immediately following, was a series of essays in which
Toynbee, having cleared the ground by laborious investigation, undertook to think out the problem further.

The essentially empirical nature of Toynbee's thought is revealed in this first effort; also the practical motivation of his historical writing, directed toward the solution of a pressing problem. "The first effect of the war was to drive one's thoughts back upon the interminable tangle of concrete problems out of which it had arisen," he wrote in the introduction to *The New Europe*. What emerged from his investigation of this "tangle" was, chiefly, the concept of "two separate organizing principles at work on the map of Europe. . . . fundamentally different in their character." [9] The two forces were Nationality and Economics. Both are fundamental, irreducible factors. To the young Toynbee, unlike the later one, nationality appeared as no evil, but as a people's self-realization, the development of its "will to cooperation." National cultures are irreducible and humanly valuable. Similarly he accepted as a given, unchangeable factor the economics of an industrial civilization. The misfortune is that most European nations attained national self-consciousness before the industrial revolution; a subsequent economic imperative often worked at cross-purposes to nationality. Perhaps the solution lies in full national self-determination plus economic rights-of-way and reciprocal trade agreements. A federation of Europe on the example of the American states offers hope. In all this Toynbee was clearly thinking in Wilsonian terms, the typical idealism of the times. Like so many others he placed hope in a League of Nations. "Why should not the State itself repeat the history of the individual?" he asked at the end of his first book. "States like individuals must eventually discover that the Bloodfeud is a burden, and that the sovereign right to wage it is not Liberty but a mockery of it." [10] At the age of twenty-six Toynbee had thus written two important books dealing with the most vital theme of the times, books which indicated as yet no great originality of thought, but which stamped him as a young scholar of accomplished craftsmanship, strong interpretative powers, and a gifted pen.

Commentator on World Affairs

Toynbee's work with the Foreign Office led him to Versailles, where he served on the British Delegation (Middle Eastern section) at the peace conference.[11] There he suffered from the ghastly confusion and duplicity of Allied policy toward the Middle East, a familiar story that included broken promises to the Arabs and a Franco-British imperialist "deal." It is also evident that Toynbee's rather unworldly idealism was shocked at the contact with political methods in the Paris cockpit. Still, the experience plainly broadened and matured him. He mingled with the great of whom at least one, Jan Smuts, was to leave a strong imprint on his thought. Then in 1919, just thirty years old, he was offered a chair newly endowed at the University of London by some Greeks in England, the Koraes professorship of Byzantine and Modern Greek language.

Dr. Burrow, the Principal of King's College, took a keen interest in the Chair, and looked about him for a Professor who should have not merely the gift of scholarship, but the zeal and breadth of view which might make the subject of the chair a source of vital intellectual interest in the University, and to some extent, a bond between Great Britain and Greece. He approached a young Fellow of Balliol, an historian and scholar of unusual brilliance, who had travelled on foot through the greater part of Greece, talking intimately to the peasants in their own language, and who had in 1919 lately returned from work for the Foreign Office at the Peace Conference. . . . Mr. Toynbee was also known as the editor of the voluminous mass of evidence in the possession of Lord Bryce about the Armenian massacres which took place during the war, and had contributed an important social and historical study of the genesis and method of such massacres.[12]

Having been assured that he need not confine himself to Language but might continue to pursue his historical interests, and also that this was not an endowment for propaganda purposes, he eagerly accepted. The next few years were fruitful ones. When hostilities broke out between Greece and Turkey after the peace settlement, Toynbee secured a leave of absence to go to the area, gaining journalistic privileges by becoming a correspondent for the *Manchester Guardian*. During most of the year 1921 he accompanied the Greek armies. When they advanced into Asia Minor, he found an unusual opportunity to apply his knowledge of both languages (Greek and Turkish) and to gratify his intense curiosity about the social forces at work on these people. When an international committee inquired into alleged massacres of Turks by the advancing Greeks, it was Toynbee who was instrumental in uncovering evidence of this which otherwise, it seems, would have gone undetected.

The Western Question in Greece and Turkey emerged from these experiences; it was easily his best book so far, a brilliant piece of analysis which won wide attention. Toynbee had immersed himself in this question through experience and study. What came out was a] a bitter indictment of Western diplomacy, and the peace settlement, the indifference and ineptitude of which on Toynbee's view had caused all this needless suffering; and b] more important, a keen study in the contact between civilizations, prophetic of his later interests. As between Greek and Turk he was nonpartisan; what he saw was the impact of Western civilization, chiefly expressed as Nationalism and as Economics, on both these peoples, destroying their old cultural equilibrium and breeding change and conflict. The moralizing cast of Toynbee's mind was in evidence, too: the book ends with a plea for mutual understanding and cooperation among civilizations. The impact of the West may not be avoided; it may possibly be constructive, but only if these other societies adopt something while retaining their individuality, and only if the West is wise enough to see that this is necessary to world peace. The meeting of peoples is primarily a spiritual problem, since it involves above all *attitudes*; it demands "that charity between members of different civilizations, without which it profiteth nothing to have the gifts of prophecy and to understand all mysteries and all knowledge." [13]

The Greeks who financed his Chair, indignant that Toynbee had shown any sympathy for the hated Turk, forced him out of it—and thus he was quickly a casualty of that lack of charity he deplored. But the book was a brilliant success. In 1925 he was offered the choice post of Director of Studies for the newly established British Institute of International Affairs (later and presently known as the *Royal* Institute of International Affairs). For the next six years his career was to be almost entirely associated with two things: the Royal Institute and the writing of his great *Study of History*. For the former he produced the yearly volumes of the *Survey of International Affairs*—the early ones written almost entirely by himself, the later ones unmistakably his own though it became necessary to assign portions to other writers. In the first year his labors accomplished the almost incredible feat of producing two massive volumes bringing international affairs up to date since 1920. The volumes were hailed with enthusiasm everywhere in the scholarly world. The same high standards continued to characterize these annual surveys down to their suspension in 1939. [14] Clarity, objectivity, detachment, careful research, and above all a flair for writing made them eagerly awaited and widely read. Such phrases as "intellectual detachment," "perspective," "penetrating analysis," "a dispassionate guide" recur in the reviews, and are clues to the tone and temper of these volumes. Necessarily sober and factual, and usually avoiding partisanship, they were yet intensely readable and stimulating; they were not mere catalogues or chronologies, but coherent surveys, subjects being arranged in a few large groups, the analysis bringing out broad developments such as reorientations of power, emergence of new policies, conflicts of states, races, and civilizations. Above all, permeating the factual accounts and the sober style was Toynbee's historical imagination, constantly finding parallels with other ages and civilizations: critics observed "a remarkable capacity for seeing historical analogies." [15]

The *Surveys* secured a worldwide reputation. Toynbee has described (in *Acquaintances*) how in 1936 Hitler gave him a two-and-a-half-hour interview (lecture) because, obviously, he knew how influential Toynbee's yearbook was—this just prior to the Rhineland move. Doubtless these volumes are now dated, since as contemporary accounts they necessarily failed to include much material which later came to light. But this somber Thucydidean chronicle of Western civilization during the peak of its "time of troubles" remains valuable. We have nothing today anywhere near so good as an annual survey of world affairs. Its scope and its organization of an enormous body of facts make it, technically, a truly extraordinary feat, as a yearly survey; but much more than that, its style, imagination, and flashes of insight gave it a more lasting value than any mere year-book.

Toynbee's work on *A Study of History*, which he was doing at the same time (he habitually devoted half the year to the *Surveys* and the other half to the *Study of History*), entered into a reciprocal relationship with his *Survey* work; his discoveries in the former inquiry show up in the latter, and vice versa. The two might be studied together, and in any exhaustive study of the growth of his thought should be. Passages from the *Surveys* often relate closely to motifs found in the *Study of History*. (See his own statement on the mutually fructifying effect of the two works, in *Experiences*, pp. 86–87.)

For example, an exceptional passage occurs in the 1926 volume, pp. 222–46, as an introduction to the situation in China. It is another analysis in terms of Western impact and internal breakdown. It contains the following typical Toynbee observation on the Chinese "troubles":

On the other hand it might be that these recurrent disorders were intimations of mortality—premonitions that even the Chinese "world-state" was not permanently exempt from the law of decay and dissolution which had prevailed over all similar states in the past and indeed over all human institutions. If this second explanation hit the truth, then, of course, however many times China might recover from her bouts of sickness, one bout was destined eventually to prove mortal.[16]

The conquest of Germany by Nazism brought forth, in the 1933 volume, a passage also typical of Toynbee's themes in A *Study of History*. Hitlerism appeared to him as an exaggeration and caricature of "the sinister elements which were latent in some degree in the Modern Western institution of parochial sovereignty in every one of its local embodiments";[17] that is, it was a lapse into pagan tribalism or nationalism away from the Christian heritage of a supramundane City of God, to which every Western nation is partly prone. There was a dual soul of Christianity and paganism in the West, which Germany had resolved boldly in favor of the latter.

In the 1931 volume, the opening chapter entitled "Annus Terribilis 1931," especially the first twenty-six pages, is of exceptional interest to the student of the development of Toynbee's thought. It speculates on the possibility of "a general breakdown of society"; and here, as in other places, we find that a whole section later placed in A *Study of History* was first printed almost *ipsissimis verbis* in the *Survey*.

The approach of the great European crisis from 1935 to 1939 found Toynbee in his *Survey* writings and in his public addresses rising to heights of eloquence, and sounding a grave warning against "appeasement." Objectivity still largely remains in the former, but in such a passage as the following we perceive the drift of Toynbee's thought.

The British electorate of this generation were the children of an age in which a *ci-devant* Christian Society had come to believe that its talent for clock-work (institutional as well as metallic) could dispense it from the need of holding convictions and of summoning up the courage to act upon them when the consequences of such action were likely to be unpleasant. . . . The children of the Enlightenment fell under the yoke of the Goddess Tyche or Fortune, who, under many different names, had repeatedly established her paralyzing dominion over the souls of men and women who had been called upon to live in periods of social decadence. . . . They made their momentous choice neither on the absolute criterion of morality nor on the relative criterion of expediency, but on that trivial distinction between this moment and the next which keeps the sluggard cowering between the blankets when the house is burning over his head.[18]

The same angry, hard-hitting Toynbee was heard in the Chatham House address of January 1939, after Munich, an address which gives an insight into his philosophy:

It seems to me that there are really only two possible ideals for mankind. . . . If a man is not going to be a man of power constructively in the world, then he must aim at being a man of thought or art, or at being a saint. But a man or a country that gives up the one ideal without embracing the other is irretrievably lost.[19]

The dualism that Toynbee has always tended to see in human affairs—City of God and City of Man—has its piquant counterpart in the oscillation of his own historical work between objective analysis and fervent moralizing. The latter kept breaking in during the tense months preceding World War II.

During these years, when not occupied with the Surveys, Toynbee, now a Research Professor of International

History at the University of London, worked on his huge *Study of History*, the first three volumes of which appeared in 1934, the second three in 1939. The plan of the book had apparently come to him as early as 1921, though he began serious work only in 1927 and actual writing in 1930.[20] Toynbee's other earlier writings ought to be mentioned briefly before proceeding to a discussion of his magnum opus. He has had a persistent interest in classical Greece; he contributed a chapter to the *Legacy of Greece* symposium, and himself edited and translated two volumes of Greek literature.[21] No one who has read any of A *Study of History* can fail to see the enormous influence on Toynbee of Hellenic thought, which had been the core of his "old-fashioned" education and which was his first intellectual love, learned at the feet of such scholars as Gilbert Murray and A. E. Zimmern. The influence is both specific and general, providing him with a good share of his larger philosophy as well as with a store of metaphor and illusion.[22] One could speculate that the essential structure of Toynbee's history, as has been said of Thucydides', is that of Greek tragedy.[23] It has been noted that his model for the breakdown of civilizations is the Hellenic case.

He also had contributed a chapter on Greece to an earlier cooperative history of the Balkans, and in 1926 he published, with a coauthor, a history of Turkey.[24] In A *Study of History*, as the reader can easily see, it is in these fields—Greece, Turkey, and to some extent the whole Islamic world—that Toynbee is strongest; these he knows thoroughly, and is no mere amateur relying on secondary sources, as in other fields of history he must necessarily be.

Perhaps no other of Toynbee's lesser writings before 1939 is important enough to merit special comment in a brief study, unless it would be his informal travel book, A *Journey to China*, which appeared in 1931 (London: Constable and Co. Ltd.), the record of a long trip made the previous year, during which he met the Chiang Kai-sheks. Since Toynbee was beginning the writing of

A *Study of History* at this time and took advantage of this journey to learn a great deal at first hand about China and Japan, it ought to be recorded as a significant experience. In later years he continued the habit of writing about his travels, obviously to him a prime means of historical education.[25]

This, then, was the background of the mind which undertook the staggering task of writing an analytic world history. Toynbee had watched his own Western civilization in trouble, torn by the problem of conflicting national sovereignties and apparently all but bankrupt of creative responses to this problem; he had observed and analyzed its impact on other civilizations; he had pondered on the analogies between this and other breakdowns of civilizations; he had become intimately acquainted with at least three other great civilized traditions. If he started by wondering how civilizations fell, and why (and with the knowledge that there had been many civilizations, of which most had died), he would be led naturally to ask, what precisely is a civilization? How many have there been? How did they rise, how grow, how decline and fall? And what general conclusion may we draw from this gigantic drama? To nothing less than the answer to these questions he addressed himself.

A Study of History, 1–6

Toynbee's magnum opus begins with some comments, under the heading of "The Relativity of Historical Thought," on the tendency of modern historiography to undergo an "industrialization" in which the act of synthesis is lost. Not only industrialism but nationalism has laid heavy hands on history, Toynbee reflects. As for the former influence, it has made historians marvelously skillful in mechanical ways, and in organization of research, but at the cost of compartmentalization;

life is not seen "whole," and great historical intellects
—he instances Mommsen—have turned their talents
largely to the laborious technicalities of research, or like
Acton have failed to write the creative synthesis they
yearned to write. He criticizes the dictation of research
by the presence of materials: the Seleucid empire neg-
lected while the Egyptian exploited endlessly, simply
because material has been preserved for the latter,
though from the standpoint of world development the
former is surely much more interesting. Here is the
apology which any such project as Toynbee's requires in
this day and age: the task is impossible and yet it must
be attempted.

So far as the influence of nationalism is concerned, it
has led, Toynbee thinks, to the taking of a false field of
synthesis even when such is undertaken. In various ways
and for various reasons scholars have adopted nations as
the units of study, "partly by professional experience,
partly by a psychological conflict [the need for some
sort of unity] and partly by the general spirit of their
age." [26] But the nation, he submits, is not an "intelligible unit of study." This is, rather, the "society" or
civilization. If the attempt is made to find the proper
unit or field by looking, say, at English history, one dis-
covers that the unit of which England is a part and
without which its history cannot be understood reaches
out in space to embrace the whole of a Western or
European civilization which emerged after the fall of
Rome. It is therefore with "societies" that Toynbee
proposes to deal as his units of historical study.

His first task, then, is to identify his societies. Seeking
their criteria, he finds a clue in that relationship of
"apparentation-and-affiliation" which obtained between
the Western society and the earlier Hellenic society of
which it was the offspring, and which also obtained
between this same parent and another offspring, the
Orthodox Christian society. There is a modern Islamic
society which on examination turns out to be the union
of two societies, Iranic and Arabic; but these two were

themselves affiliates of an older society which may be traced back to an original Syriac society. He has begun to develop criteria by which societies can be identified. There is always a "universal state," which has been preceded by a "time of troubles" when strife between political fractions of the society raged until an intolerable situation was cured by the final conquest of all by one and the imposition of a *pax Romanica*. This stage of the universal state is a stage in the process of decline, however, and the relief it brings is but a brief period of "Indian Summer"; it is followed by the development of an internal and an external proletariat alienated from its traditions and dominant class. The typical achievement of the internal proletariat is a higher religion leading to a "universal church"; of the external proletariat, barbarian war bands and a *Völkerwanderung*. Out of these two elements are forged the new affiliated civilization or society. Examining all existing societies—India and China as well as those mentioned—and probing backward in their histories with these criteria in mind, Toynbee at length drew up a list of all the civilizations, living and dead, which he could discover.[27] There were six original or unaffiliated civilizations, of which two (the Egyptiac and the Andean) left no progeny and four (Sinic, Minoan, Sumeric, Mayan) did. Four more (Hittite, Syriac, Indic?, Hellenic?—the last two questionable in Toynbee's view) were apparently "infra-affiliated," which we may translate as more remotely descended from a parent-civilization (no universal church tie). Six (Western, Orthodox Christian, Far Eastern, Iranic, Arabic, Hindu) are affiliates, while three more (Babylonic, Yucatec, Mexic) Toynbee called "supra-affiliated" since the inheritance was greater and the tie closer with the parent. To these nineteen he added, as fairly distinct societies, the Russian offshoot of the Orthodox Christian society and the Japanese-Korean offshoot of the Far Eastern society, making a total of twenty-one.

Toynbee must next demonstrate that these societies

widely separated in time and space are comparable, or subject to comparative analysis. He here attacks the idea of the "Unity of History"—that is, a single mighty torrent. The European idea that there is really only one civilization is an enormous error explicable, he believes, by three great misconceptions: the egocentric illusion, the catchword of the "unchanging East," and the misconception of growth as a movement in a straight line. Thus he proceeds to establish to his own satisfaction, replying to as many objections as he can think of, that these societies are classifiable and comparable.

Having cleared the ground he can proceed to the comparative analysis of civilizations. The first problem, naturally, is that of their geneses: how are they created? In that eternal rhythm of Static and Dynamic, or in the Chinese term which Toynbee borrows, "Yin and Yang," a very long Yin stage of primitivism, the length of which is explicable in terms of *vis inertiae* or the holding on to an integration which works, has been broken in the last mere six thousand years by the dynamism of civilization. What has caused this stirring? In accordance with his usual method Toynbee examines and rejects a number of hypotheses, seeking to find his way via this critical process to an acceptable explanation. Displaying a considerable knowledge of anthropology, he rejects the racial explanation (1, pp. 227–49). This explanation of "some special quality of Race in some fraction of mankind" as the origin of civilization is "either an ineptitude or a fraud." Next, God is rejected as a source of civilization. If race is too trivial a cause, God is too great: He can exist as transcendent first cause or as Bergsonian creative immanence (Toynbee's view, no doubt, is the latter), but, being practically coexistent with Life itself, God could not have been "an impetus to a part of Mankind and not to the whole" (1, p. 249). There remains the environmental explanation. But this too is inadequate, though it provides a clue to the true answer. In this passage where he quarrels respectfully with the environmentalists, Toynbee tries to show that "a virtually identical combination of the two elements in the environment (human and non-human) may give birth to a civilization in one instance and fail to give birth in another instance, without our being able to account for the difference in the outcome" by any environmental factors (1, p. 269). Conversely, civilizations have emerged in environments "utterly diverse." With this view few historians or anthropologists would quarrel.

He arrives at the view that environment exerts an influence, but cannot explain all. It is the Challenge; a Response may or may not be elicited. What determines this? It is in the last analysis beyond prediction, Toynbee answers; it is P. A. Means's "x-factor"; it is the human element, and here Toynbee returns to something expressed earlier, the conviction that the "apathetic fallacy," an illusion of scientific certainty or of human determinism, has too much taken hold of historians. There is no need to look for a uniformity in this motif or challenge-and-response, any more than in a battle or a bridge game. On the analogy of a battle, one may know the forces, the strategy, the equipment, yet fail to predict the outcome, for what men will do under actual battle conditions is always uncertain. Perhaps inconsistently but steadily, Toynbee has insisted on the essential unpredictability and indeterminacy of history.

Turning to an investigation of the various geneses of civilization, he examines them in terms of challenge-and-response. The challenge has varied; it may have been climatic change bringing desiccation, as it was to the Afrasian grasslanders, or, as it was to the Mayans, the challenge of rain and forest. In any event Toynbee rejects the thesis that civilizations are engendered in an opulent environment where life is exceptionally easy. With a host of examples he makes the point that the most fruitful condition is one wherein a challenge is presented that is severe enough to demand a response on pain of death, yet not so severe that it cannot be met, or discourages response by its hopelessness. Civilization is never a product of the lotus lands; it has often arisen under the stimulus of immense adversity; it does not arise, however, unless the challenge is within the golden mean of "enough and not too much." To the stimulus of "hard ground" as a factor in eliciting creative responses in history Toynbee adds others: the stimuli of "new ground," of "blows," of pressures, and of penalization. (The Jew serves as an apt illustration of the last.) In volume 2 under the general heading of "Genesis" he also discusses some "abortive" civilizations, such as the early medieval Irish Christian and the Scandinavian, which were "nipped in the bud" by being subjected to insuperable difficulties before their civilization was well established.

Volume 3 launches on the next problem, that of Growth. Toynbee begins by emphasizing that in the sense of civilization, growth is not something that automatically follows on birth, instancing some "arrested" civilizations which were born but never grew. Like climbers on a cliff, who have reached a position where they can just hang on but cannot climb further, these civilizations represent examples of a challenge not quite too severe to be met, yet too severe to leave any margin at all for further social growth. They are doomed to a "fatal rigidity," a "perilous immobility at high tension." Such are the Eskimos, the Nomads, the Polynesians, and, in terms of a challenge which was not physical but human the 'Osmanlis (Ottoman Turks) and the Spartans. We have noted that on Turkish ground Toynbee is apt to be at his best; the rest of this is also remarkably stimulating. Among other things this discussion provides him with the opportunity to venture afield in such domains as biology and literary utopias, in pursuit of the idea that stability can exist at the cost of sterilization or spiritual death.

Thus growth is not inevitable, but can stop. What makes it go on? For one thing, he has been led now to conceive that

the real optimum challenge is rather one which not only stimulates the challenged party to achieve a single successful response but also stimulates him to acquire a momentum that carries him on a step farther: from achievement to a fresh struggle, from the solution of one problem to the presentation of another, from momentary rest to reiterated movement. (3, p. 119)

There must be an "*élan* which carries the challenged party through equilibrium into an overbalance which exposes him to a fresh challenge," and so on indefinitely. Toynbee quotes Walt Whitman: "It is provided in the essence of things that from any fruition of success, no matter what, shall come forth something to make a greater struggle necessary." It is his version of the dialectical movement of history.[28]

What is the nature of growth? Once again we are shown two false hypotheses before arriving at the author's version of the true one. As concomitants or criteria of growth he rejects   a] increasing command over the human environment and   b] increasing command over the physical environment. Neither geographic expansion nor technological progress will stand scrutiny as evidences of real growth. Geographic expansion is more often, indeed, an evidence of "social disease," Toynbee will go so far as to say (wherein he agreed with Oswald Spengler, to whom modern European imperialism was a sign of decay). It is "the malady of the Reptiles, who turned huge on the eve of being surpassed by the Mammals; or the malady of Goliath, who grew to gigantic stature in order to succumb to David" (3, p. 153). As for technology, it has on numerous occasions progressed while civilization as a whole declined. Here, as always, of course, Toynbee appears to draw his conclusions from a mass of historical evidence, ranging far and wide over human history for his examples. He arrives at a conclusion which has really been implicit in his previous criticism of the other hypotheses: the truest concomitant of growth is "etherialization" or "spiritualization," a movement inward from the macrocosm to the microcosm, a realization that treasure is to be laid up in the soul and not in gold or goods. The essence of the thought is contained in a quotation from "The Lay of the Battle of Maldon" on the title page:

> Thought shall be the harder,
> Heart the keener,
> Mood shall be the more,
> As our might lessens.

The Decadents of the 1890s had thought that an exquisite literature is the consolation of a dying culture. Toynbee seems to hold that it is the product of a civilization at its zenith. This preponderance of "thought," "heart," and "mood" in a growing civilization means, in turn, a capacity for self-determination: a civilization while still in health and growth knows where it is going and determines its own destiny, and conversely one of the signs of breakdown is a loss of this power of self-determination.

An analysis of growth follows. Herein Toynbee draws heavily on Smuts and others for a theory of the relation between society and the individual, and he draws on the man whose philosophy perhaps influenced him more than any other, Henri Bergson, for the concept of the creative individual. Progress is not automatic or unconscious; it is by specific acts of individual creation, which are essentially artistic or even mystic. "It is only the thrust of genius that has ever forced the inertia of Humanity to yield," said Bergson.[29] But under certain social conditions even the "thrust of genius" may not be enough. The social situation determines whether the creative genius will be accepted or rejected.

The creative process Toynbee sees as symbolized in a motif of withdrawal-and-return (Plato's famed metaphor). The path of the creative genius who returns from his mystic experience "trailing clouds of glory" is traced in brief vignettes of the lives of a variety of great men, from Jesus and Paul to Garibaldi and Lenin, including also Confucius, Ibn Khaldun, and a "pleiad of historians." This creative role may be played by whole communities as well as individuals, as Athens was the "education of Hellas." This, then, is the way growth occurs: a creative minority is imitated by an uncreative majority, though in this lies a danger. Finally, Toynbee points to a consequence of growth in *differentiation*: at its apex each civilization has a distinctive style and ethos, sharply defined. This, too, is an echo of Oswald Spengler's *Decline of the West*. But Toynbee quarrels with Spengler's absolute relativism of all thought to a particular civilization. His Christian universalism and his faith in both final truth and the possibility of a general human progress separates Toynbee from Spengler here as elsewhere.

The fourth and perhaps a most exciting volume deals with the breakdowns of civilizations. "The problem of the breakdowns of civilizations," he says in a morose and sharply etched introduction, "stares us in the face" (4, p. 4). We are too close to it to say anything about our own civilization with assurance; but all signs indicate that we are far into our "time of troubles" and on the road of breakdown. The nature of the breakdowns of civilizations has already been indicated in the preceding books: it is "a failure of creative power in the minority, an answering withdrawal of mimesis on the part of the majority, and a consequent loss of social unity in the society as a whole" (4, p. 6). As for the cause, that is a problem which the author once more approaches indirectly through his familiar method of examining and rejecting some well-known theories. He quarrels with Spengler (inevitable life cycles on the analogy of the human organism), with Plato (racial degeneration), and with the ubiquitous idea of recurring cycles expressed by Shelley in his famous line in *Hellas*, "The world's great age begins anew." There is a rhythm, but it is not pure repetition. There is no necessity of a civilization's dying, as there is of a man's; for "the divine spark of creative activity is instinct in ourselves" (4, p. 39). So far as concerns more specific theories of breakdown, Toynbee examines and rejects the idea that it is basically due to loss of command over the environment, whether human or physical, strongly challenging Gibbon's famous verdict on Rome.

Toynbee's final verdict is suicide. Breakdown is caused by self-failure, he would claim, every time; it is due to a fatal weakness or failure of response; "we are betrayed by what is false within." But there are forces which develop as a civilization ages which tend to make the likelihood of the creative response slimmer. The "mechanicalness of mimesis" has already been suggested as an Achilles heel of every civilization. More than that, institutions are intractable. Here he seems to approach what sociologists call the "cultural lag," or what Trotsky laid down as a law of uneven historical development. The dead weight of old institutions gets in the way when a new challenge is presented; it is hard to pour new wine in old bottles. There is, moreover, the eternal tendency to "rest on one's oars," and also to "idolize" a past self or a past technique or a past institution, to believe that what worked once will always work. Many examples of such intractability and such fatal "idolization of an ephemeral past" are given. Finally Toynbee goes to his Greeks for the concept of tragedy as consisting in the deadly path from *Koros* to *Hybris* to *Atē*— from arrogance to utter infatuation. Of this fatal "intoxication of victory," the most grievous and lethal manifestation is militarism, which is "suicidal." Thus ends the most memorable volume of *A Study of History*, with Toynbee at *his* creative zenith when describing—significantly—the process of breakdown.

The problem of the fifth volume is Disintegration—which is a step beyond Breakdown, but seems not to follow inevitably any more than growth inevitably follows genesis. Just as some were "arrested" after birth, examples exist of societies which after embarking on a breakdown have remained for centuries in a petrified state, the prime one being ancient Egypt. Provided the path from breakdown to disintegration continues, the dominant motif and criterion of the latter stage is Schism—an outward schism in the body social which has its counterpart in an inward schism in the souls of individuals. The social schism is typically both vertical and horizontal. As for the latter, a *ci-devant* creative minority which the masses willingly followed has become an uncreative ruling-class which holds sway by force or fraud, and this is answered in time by an act of secession on the part of an internal proletariat which recognizes the bankruptcy of its masters. This is the peculiar phenomenon of disintegration; for the vertical schism (interstate warfare) is only the abuse of an articulation into communities which already existed, and indeed exists everywhere and at all times.

The other important social factor is an *external* proletariat, in the form of those outlying barbarians who, in the civilization's creative stage, were being absorbed into it, charmed and converted by its superior qualities; they now secede also, and become foes rather than converts, unwilling rather than willing subjects.

The "dominant [uncreative] minority" is not quite altogether devoid of creativeness; its one great contribution is the universal state, and this achievement of political efficiency which gives the beleaguered society a spell of peace, Toynbee concedes, is not lacking in value. The dominant minority in the latter stages of decay also gives rise, typically, to a significant philosophy—Stoicism, Confucianism, Buddhism. But by far the greatest creative act of the disintegrative phase is that of the internal proletariat, which produces, at length, a higher religion, after having experimented fruitlessly in cults of revolutionary violence. On such a view present-day communism of the Marxian vintage becomes a religion whose error is its violence and which despite valid and promising elements is doomed thereby to frustration. The role of the external proletariat is mainly destructive, but creative elements of poetry (the epic, the folk saga) and even religion can come from it.

In transferring his attention from outer to inner world, from Schism in the Body Social to an organically related Schism in the Soul, Toynbee tries to generalize about ideas, modes of behavior and feeling in a declining society where creative action is frustrated. These he splits into antithetical pairs which are alternative substitutes for creative action. Such, on the plane of personal behavior, are the polar extremes of abandon and ascetism; on the plane of feeling, the "sense of drift" and the "sense of sin." On the plane of social life, there are two pairs of ways in which, on Toynbee's view, men may respond to and attempt to deal with the problems posed by a disintegrating society. One pair is violent, or inevitably eventuates in violence; these are the remedies of "archaism" and "futurism" or the reactionary and the revolutionary as one might call them. Both attempt to escape from an intolerable present by the tour de force of turning back the clock or setting it ahead; to Toynbee both are escapes from creative activity and are doomed to bloody failure.

The gentle pair comprises the responses of Detachment and Transfiguration. (A relation exists in that the archaist is said to be prone to turn into the disciple of detachment while the disillusioned futurist may become the apostle of transfiguration). Detachment is largely the goal of that dominant-minority philosophy previously mentioned; its votaries are the Stoics and Buddhists, in modern terms doubtless the Schopenhauerians and the esthetes, whose way is the way of withdrawal into an inner imperturbability with its logical goal an utter Nirvana. To Toynbee this achievement of the philosophers is sublime but sterile. It leads nowhere, socially speaking; it is withdrawal without return.

The discussion of the sense of promiscuity and of drift as symptoms of social illness are interesting portions of this final volume. The differentiation of a sharp and specific style, art, language, literature, thought which is characteristic of the growth phase gives way to cultural fuzziness, incoherence, promiscuity, standardization. Yet this vulgar confusion of values has its compensation in a sense of unity which it breeds and in which the higher religion may flourish. The mingling of gods and of peoples is an indispensable prelude, as many before Toynbee realized, to that higher religion which embraces all of mankind in a single brotherhood under a God who is no longer the patron deity of a tribe but is a loving Father to all men.

Having analyzed the failures of Archaism, Futurism, and Detachment, it only remains for Toynbee to bring forward Transfiguration as the solution. Having exposed the fatal defects of the Saviour with the Sword, the Saviour with the Time Machine, and the Philosopher Masked by a King, it only remains to unveil the successful creative genius as the God Incarnate in a Man, who surpasses archaist and futurist in putting aside the sword and in emphasizing a spiritual rather than a mundane kingdom, and who rises above the philosopher in returning to spread his message among the multitudes, and in promising in that message not death but life. Toynbee's sixth volume ends on a note almost of religious exaltation. The same note indeed was present in volume 5 (pp. 193–94) in the discussion of the weakness of revolutionary violence. Only by returning with a contrite heart to its Christian heritage can Western civilization avoid the fate of other vanished societies.

A Study of History, 7–10

To many of his readers the six volumes completed in 1939 comprised a satisfying unity; with the tracing of the path from growth to disintegration, and the revelation of the secret that might just enable our civilization to stave off its collapse,[30] the structure seemed complete, and the intensive discussion of Toynbee that went on in the 1940s and early 1950s—when interest in him and admiration for him was at a peak—

assumed that it was. Perhaps Toynbee should have quit when he was ahead; the subsequent volumes struck many as adding little to his thought, while perhaps reflecting a loss of literary mastery compared with the earlier ones, turning his virtue of leisurely and thorough explanation into the vice of unconscionable long-windedness. Be that as it may, Tonybee had clearly warned, in his original outline and at the end of volume 6, that more was to come. He has indicated (10, p. 237) that notes for the later volumes had been made and were put aside in safekeeping during World War II as he turned to government service. The lines that remained to be drawn had been clearly suggested. As he affirmed at the end of volume 6, the great rhythm that throbs through history, the systole and diastole which in its larger pattern manifests itself as the rise and fall of societies, is not a sterile repetition but leads somewhere; we do not, as Spengler had thought, have only so many discrete social organisms which are born and die without any significant relation to others, but rather we see that each leaves behind something which the next cycle will use. "The perpetual turning of a wheel is not a vain repetition if, at each revolution, it is carrying a vehicle that much nearer to its goal" (6, p. 374). The death throes of civilizations spawn universal states and especially universal churches. And these transcend the particular societies which give birth to them in their death agonies. We have, in short, the problem of the connections between civilizations, and the larger question of whether the whole mighty cycle of growth and decay does not constitute a single movement toward an ascertainable goal, or at least distill something of enduring value.

Toynbee resumed his labors after a delay caused by the Second World War. During the war he served as director of the Foreign Office Research Department. His work on the *Surveys*, 1946–58, has been mentioned; together with his wife (after his divorce in 1946 from Rosalind Murray) the former Veronica Boulter, who

had long assisted him at the R.I.I.A., he edited the ten
volumes covering the war and wrote portions of several
of these (see especially the fifty-page introduction to
The Eve of The War 1939).[31] The growing appreciation
of his *Study of History* also brought him opportunities
to lecture and to write more popularly, which he did not
miss; such books as *Civilization on Trial* (1948) and
The World and the West (1952), as well as numerous
magazine articles, distilled the doctrines preached in
A Study of History. (*The World and the West*, de-
livered as the Reith Lectures over the British Broad-
casting System, was substantially an abridgement of
vol. 8 of the *Study*, "Encounters between Civilizations.") The last four volumes of his *Study* came out in
1954. These were abridged by D. C. Somervell as, meanwhile, had been the first six volumes.[32]

The first part of volume 7, on Universal States is, in
bald outline, a rather pedestrian summary of the services
such states provide. Toynbee seemingly felt he had
slighted these "in treating them as mere by-products of
the disintegration of some single civilization." They are,
after all, usually accorded honor as the crowning periods
of history: the Roman Empire, or the Chinese Empire
whether under Mongol, Ming, or Manchu (which Toynbee treats as examples of alternating bouts of fever and
apathy or "rout and rally," to which universal states are
prone), or the medieval Arab Empire, or Napoleon's
Empire. Some of them lasted a very long time, though
Toynbee may insist that they merely ossified. They
supplied many services to man and they kept the peace.
In volume 7 Toynbee descends to discuss such matters
as the merits of decimal versus duodecimal systems
(and defends the Sumerian-English plan against the
rest of the world), while commenting on the useful if
mundane subjects of weights and measurements, coins
and calendars. There are digressions in this volume
about such matters as the location of capital cities, and
more obviously relevant discussions of armies and
bureaucracies and law. Accustomed by the earlier

volumes to think of these zones of history as inhabited by uncreative minorities ruling by force rather than ability, intoxicated by suicidal arrogance, and unable to escape the curse of the past, the reader may be surprised to find them now credited with much that appears creative and reasonable and successful. The Han dynasty solved the problem of the ruling minority for many centuries by co-opting its members from talented proletarians in accordance with regular procedures. The late Roman Empire "successfully obliterated" the "gulf between ruler and ruled" (7, p. 375). These points are made with Toynbee's usual charm compounded of vast erudition born elegantly on waves of metaphor and quotation, with an occasional flash of wit, the some-times ponderous circumlocutions having, en masse, a kind of hypnotic effect. At the same time we have the massive annexes for the book proper; in this case pages 569–775!

Perhaps in bringing the weight of his mind to bear on worldly matters for a time Toynbee hoped to disarm the critics who urged that he was too mystical for an historian. The last half of the long volume 7 found him returning to his more congenial manner and subject. In fact, Toynbee had changed his mind since the 1939 volumes in the direction of a greater respect for religion, not less.[33] That "religion is the serious business of the human race," [34] meant that the chief purpose of history is the distillation of the higher religions. The chief service universal states provide is the unwitting further-ance of universal churches. As the Empire sinks the Church rises, Toynbee agrees with Gibbon, but does not see the triumph as one of barbarism. Nor was the Church significant merely because it passed on the torch of civilization, serving as a chrysalis to preserve earthly civilization through a dangerous interlude. It did that in early medieval Europe, but churches do not al-ways play such a role, and their chief function is a far higher one. Churches are not the means with which to perpetuate civilization, they are themselves the highest type of civilization. Religion is the fruit of the suffering that accompanies the disintegration of secular commonwealths. Abraham emerged from the decay of Sumeric civilization, Moses from the Egyptian breakdown, and the highest prophetic expression of Judaism from the Syriac time of troubles, Toynbee maintains, in an analysis that seems oddly to make the Judaic religion not a steady development but a series of disjointed leaps, dependent on the misfortunes of others. But it did go forward; religion makes progress. And Toynbee comes close to suggesting that it is the same progress: all the great religions are much the same, he tells us— "four variations on a single theme" (7, p. 428). Eventually they may all unite in one, for they all really worship the One True God, though it looks as if Christianity will have to supply the nucleus for this unification (7, p. 440). It is the function, then, of dying civilizations to produce the universal states which in turn produce universal churches, which shelter and express, however imperfectly, the religion which grows toward perfection through generations of civilizations. That which goes forward as the wheels go around is religion. "The history of civilization turns out to be the history of religion," as Christopher Hill noted with some dismay.[35] Each religion is better than the one before, and at the close of our own age we may look forward to the "unity of mankind" and the revelation of history's meaning and purpose.

It is startling that Toynbee has thus worked his way to an idea of progress that seems almost Victorian, after beginning as the prophet of doom and the theorist of cycles (and to essentially a "straight line" view of progress, after having once denounced this as a fallacy). To be sure, the optimism was always there; as in a Proust novel, the faint germ appears early, to grow almost unsuspected until we suddenly realize what a *bouleversement* has taken place. Though formally eschewing prophecy, Toynbee in effect promises the millennial rainbow at the end of the road, in the form of one great human family united and etherealized—never destined, as he reminds us, to achieve perfection here below, but clearly to approach it as closely as is humanly possible. We are back with Tennyson, if not with Bishop Bossuet, and may feel cheated that the long journey through so many thousands of pages has landed us in so familiar a location; or perhaps gratified that the ultimate learning leads to the simplest of truths.

This was not, however, the end of Toynbee's saga, though a logical grand climax. A comparatively short section (eighty-seven pages, which for Toynbee is a bagatelle) at the beginning of volume 8 is devoted to "Heroic Ages," the other product of disintegrating civilizations, produced by the external proletariat. The barbarians who live outside the frontiers of a civilization are subject to its attraction during the creative phase of that civilization, but during its disintegration they absorb only the sinister aspects of its culture while becoming alienated from it. Put rather pretentiously in the form of "laws," Toynbee's point is that the barbarians are likely to adopt the culture of a higher civilization in distorted form, the more distorted as this civilization itself loses its structural harmony and becomes a victim of dysfunction and anomie. We are given an interesting explanation of the myths and sagas of heroic ages as rising from that psychological crisis felt by the barbarian when he is in transit from tribalism to civilization, when his primitive psyche has been jolted by the impact of civilization. For the brutal integrity of the Heroic Age barbarians Toynbee has no Nietzschean admiration; he does not see them as renewers of vital energy but simply as destroyers, and the so-called Heroic Age was really only a "sordid interlude" between civilizations. Yet in their small way the barbarians may contribute to the development of the higher religions, for they too may be chrysalises functioning as the means of transmission from one civilization to another. Indeed, we see that those civilizations which were affiliated to their parent civilizations chiefly through external proletariats (Hellenic, Syriac, Indic) stood a better chance of success than those affiliated through dominant minorities (Babylonic, Yucatec, Mexic). (Toynbee later dropped the view that these last societies were independent of their predecessors at all. On his own evidence, we might readily infer that barbarians provide a renewal of vital energy; but no such conclusion is drawn.) This, however, was only true of the second generation barbarians (i.e., those who came after the earliest civilization, the post-Minoan barbarians in the case of Greece), not the third, in which category stand the Germanic barbarians of the European Dark Ages; the latter, on Toynbee's view, contributed nothing except a little poetry and mythology. He is committed to the view that Christianity was created and carried by the Roman "internal proletariat," while the "external proletariat" proved savagely sterile. A critic might be tempted to wonder whether such "barbarians" as Charles Martel and Charlemagne did not prove the most useful of Christians. But we shall leave the innumerable criticisms of Toynbee to the next chapter; in this one the only purpose is to expound him.

"Encounters between Civilizations in Space," which occupies the bulk of volume 8 is largely a study of the ways in which various other civilizations have reacted to Western civilization. Partly abandoning the view that his societies or civilizations are so many discrete monads, Toynbee declares that in their final stage we cannot understand them except through their interaction with other societies. To study the sum of these interactions would be a large order, Toynbee admits. (A more pedestrian historian might shrink from the task of writing a history of the contacts between any two major nations, say France and England; Toynbee proposes to write about the contacts of all societies with all others.) He decides to begin with the encounters between Modern Western Civilization and other civilizations. (We have not heretofore heard about the need to periodize Western civilization, which has been treated all of a piece; indeed, the division of it into periods was singled out for criticism in volume 1. But now there is an excursion in which it is decided that the modern period began toward the end of the fifteenth century.) Several studies then take up the impact of the modern West on Russia, on Turkey, on Islamic society, on India, on the Jews, and on the Far East, while others deal with the contacts of medieval Europe with Syria and Byzantium, followed by a section on the Hellenistic minglings of civilized traditions and some others. These are often perceptive, and contain passages of vivid narrative such as Toynbee is capable of intruding, perhaps incongruously, into his analytical structure. The trouble is that this segment seems to dangle from the rest of the *Study*, and, secondly, to comprise an all too inadequate survey of its enormous subject. While this may be said of the rest of the *Study* too, of course, the magnificence of its conception and structure leads us to suspend our criticisms while reading. Here, in what amounts to a special study of one field, the interactions between societies, we become more conscious of the inadequacies.

Nevertheless, if Toynbee has no more than scratched a surface, it is an intriguing surface and the scratches are occasionally incisive. The conclusions reached are perhaps not very startling. If a society is the victim of an assault by an aggressive or "radioactive" challenger, it may meet force by force, or it may respond pacifically, or it may be stimulated to a spiritual or ideological response, or it may do all of these. (If a stranger aggresses against me, I can punch him in the nose, I can walk away from him, or I can try creatively to "relate" to him as a friend.) It may try to isolate itself, or it may adopt the strategy of imitation. It may breed "Zealots" who prefer desperate measures to any sacrifice of cultural and political autonomy, or "Herodians" who bend with the wind and adapt to the aggressor's ways (examples derived of course from Rome and the Jews). The impact of one civilization on another may be destructive to the recipient of the cultural influences (e.g., industrialism and nationalism exported from the West work havoc in some non-Western cultures). It also may produce damaging arrogance and racism in the aggressive society.

The conclusion of this section is a typical one. Toynbee relates the "Zealots" who fanatically combat all alien influence to the Archaists of volume 5—they unrealistically cling to the past—while the "Herodians" are Futurists who would leap too hastily into the unknown. Paul, who passed from Zealotism to Christianity without thereby becoming an Herodian, represents the creative, spiritual path. He preached neither Judaism nor Hellenism, but a new way which drew on both; and thus the challenge of cultural invasion may call forth a response which is genuinely creative and, of course, religious. (See the section on Paul in 3, pp. 263–64.)

"Contacts between Civilizations in Time" is a survey of some Renaissances (first part of vol. 9). It contains some remarkable judgments, very dogmatically presented and seemingly perverse when compared with the usual construction of European history; for Toynbee will not concede that the use of past materials by a civilization is other than black magic with the most appalling results. Renaissances are like Archaisms, the only difference being that the former borrow from a previous civilization, not from the past of the same civilization. (Since to Toynbee Hellenism was not the dawn of Western civilization but a different civilization to which we are only apparented, the various Renaissances of European history are cases of remembering the ghost of an ancestor.) Now in European history as it is normally presented, medieval Europe's recovering of Hellenic and Roman culture (which it had in fact never quite lost) was a good thing. In its unsteady and barbarous infancy, Germanic Europe did well to strengthen its ties with a more civilized past, to renew contact with the Mediterranean from which all civilization flowed. Charlemagne's momentary achievement in restoring something like the old Roman Empire was a pillar thrust up out of the marsh of barbarism, which perhaps saved Europe from sinking irretrievably into that marsh; the twelfth- and thirteenth-century reception of Aristotelianism and other elements of Greek thought was a landmark of intellectual progress; the Italian Renaissance of the fourteenth and fifteenth century completed the education of adolescent Europe at the hands of the ancients and prepared the way for its growth to political and cultural maturity. Something like this is the usual version, but Toynbee will have none of it.[36] He rejoices at Charlemagne's failure, finds that Aristotelianism halted the creativity of Western thought, and deplores that dark necromancy by which the Italians revived the ancient city-states—an ominous introduction to modern statism and nationalism. This view, a most debatable one, is set forth with a harshness and bitterness that is unlike Toynbee and may show the cloven hoof of the religious zealot; for what he sees in the Roman Empire and the Renaissance State and even Greek philosophy is the seed of modern paganism, which ultimately issued in war and totalitarianism. We are obviously in the presence of a strong moral or ideological judgment.[37]

The remainder of volume 9 takes up anew the question of whether human affairs are ruled by law, or whether, in the words of H. A. L. Fisher which seem to have haunted and intensely annoyed Toynbee, history has no "plot, rhythm, or predetermined pattern" but is only "the play of the contingent and the unforeseen." This gives him a chance to review his findings. Through a number of *longueurs* he remains convinced that regularities may be found in human history, that he has discovered many of these, that they are especially pronounced in the declining stages of civilizations; but that there is no reason to suppose that "an unprecedented spiritual advance" cannot avert the fate that seemingly awaits Western civilization. For God offers a degree of freedom to his children, if they will but take it. On pages 395–405, Toynbee comes close to approving a Manichean or Gnostic religious philosophy in which a God of Good struggles in nature and history with a malevolent or amoral principle—a view which he has elsewhere indicated is indeed his own (cf. Aron, pp. 20–21). But at the end of the next section, on the present state and prospects of Western civilization, he permits himself the optimistic hope that mechanization will leave men freer to "fulfill the true end of Man by glorifying God and enjoying Him once again" (9, p. 640). And this, we would have to say midway of the twentieth century, is optimism indeed.

It is—to repeat—difficult to escape the feeling that Toynbee has slipped in the last four volumes; outwardly the apparatus looks the same, but the indefinable magic has gone, and the excitement of the quest which permeates the earlier volumes has given way to a dogged determination to finish the job. But this may be in part a subjective reaction on our part. The years between 1939 and 1954 had given us time to absorb the Toynbee effect and become to a degree immune to it. The message was no longer new; most of the last four volumes embroidered on themes already laid down. The religious stress which made a magnificent climax in volume 6 now became somewhat cloying. There is less unity in the late volumes, which often seem to wander without much direction. The erudition is as dazzling as ever, but now occasionally looks superfluous and showy; the style is trademarked Toynbee, but can sometimes sound like self-parody, or—in the great historian's own terminology—mechanical mimesis has replaced genuine creativity. Nevertheless, the last volumes present most clearly his basic conception of the historical process, that progress takes place through the distillation of ever more advanced religions by way of successive generations of civilizations, and in no other way; that the turning of the wagon wheel does take us further down the road. And they continue to overwhelm us with the sheer weight of their knowledge, which is used to support challenging generalizations of the largest sort, and which is communicated by the constantly allusive and metaphoric style.

The most interesting portion of the last volume (10),

which contains the index and some miscellaneous comments on history and historians (which students usually find interesting as a discussion of the motives, inspirations, and method of historians but which looks like a whole volume of these annexes tacked on to each of the other volumes, material flowing from his copious pen which escaped the boundaries of his argument and was relegated to the rear), is perhaps the long list of "Acknowledgements and Thanks," almost an intellectual autobiography. His mother, Gibbon, Freeman, and numerous other well-known historians (among them F. J. Teggart, A. E. Zimmern, the great Rostovtzeff, Prescott, and, surprisingly, Sir Lewis Namier, whose view of history was so utterly different from Toynbee's),[38] are joined by others—childhood books, vistas of scenery, classical writers (Plato, Lucretius, Polybius), novels; a long list, including even the Rockefeller Foundation. Among general intellectual influences we are not surprised by Bergson, St. Augustine, Ibn Khaldun,[39] Aeschylus, Goethe, and the Bible; nor should we be by Carl Jung, though this has not been mentioned. Who more than the great Swiss explorer of the unconscious has done more to convince modern man that, in order to heal his divided soul, he must return to religion and nourish his psyche on the great myths of mankind? Toynbee constantly uses myth for his metaphors: Yin and Yang, Prometheus, Faust, Job, and so forth.[40] He tells us that he found Challenge and Response in Robert Browning.[41] The whole remarkable section is a tribute to Toynbee's piety, and also perhaps to his naïveté. He is under a compulsion to tell us everything, he can hold nothing back. Such is the man, and such is his work.

2

The Criticism of Toynbee's History

If it is difficult to encircle the mighty girth of Toynbee's writings in a short survey (as we tried to do in chapter 1), it is even harder to take account of all the criticism he has received. The reasons for this should be evident but are worth brief comment. Toynbee had touched on virtually every area and period of history each of which today is inhabited by specialists who are bound to know more, in most cases, than he did; his gargantuan curiosity had carried him far beyond the range of anyone's, even a Toynbee's, possible mastery. The cries of outraged specialists, it may be worth noting, were not evoked simply by Toynbee's factual errors, but by his fantastic (to them) interpretations. To put it one way, his was a view from a mountaintop, which saw things far differently from those laboring in the fields below. What they saw he did not see, and what he saw they did not see. Some praised his different perspective as uniquely valuable.[1] But Toynbee's perspective led him to seemingly odd interpretations, by the standards of more earthbound historians, when he dealt with specific episodes or processes of history. Critics would say he forced them into his arbitrary pattern; Toynbee could reply that everyone must have a pattern; yet clearly his was most unusual. In any case, we have Toynbee at war with the specialist historians. Since he impinged on other fields, the assailants were not confined to historians. They came from a good many other disciplines but most especially from Religion, since Toynbee had set himself up as a student of comparative religion, an interpreter of all religions, even a theologian. Here, obviously, he was something of an inspired amateur, encroaching on fields well guarded by professionals.

Philosophically, Toynbee's whole method raised doubts. Was he guilty of applying scientific positivism, wrongly, to the domain of human affairs? Were his generalizations and "laws" really valid? If not, was this because he had erred in carrying out a legitimate program, or was the whole program falsely conceived? What about his frankly moralizing position? Questions that normally haunt the theory of history, including whether history can be an exact science, whether it can or should generalize, whether it should pronounce moral judgments, in what its value and its status as "explanation" consist, all came up for review. Philosophers as well as theoretically inclined historians and social scientists were interested in these questions. One finds Toynbee discussed in philosophical journals. (In recent years both philosophers and historians have become more interested in theory of history.)

Toynbee had also entered the lists as commentator on current civilization. He affronted the liberals by his frank religiosity and they accused him of obscurantism and anti-intellectualism. He affronted conservatives by his pacifism and internationalism, together with a certain sententious and misty idealism in politics. While, in the atmosphere of the Cold War, some accused him of gentleness toward communism and betrayal of the West, the Marxists scorned him as a purveyor of shoddy historical goods and a mortal foe of communism. The Jews entered into a particularly bitter controversy with A Study of History because of its treatment of Judaism; but Christians generally found Toynbee hopelessly unorthodox, too. Beyond this, he invited discussion of basic political questions of all sorts: the role of the state, the problem of war, the destiny and condition of modern man.

Meanwhile others talked about his style, his prolixity, his conceit, his naïveté, his self-righteousness. His defenders might admit the imperfections yet see his vast work as an awe-inspiring monument. Few questioned his greatness even as they assailed his system. In the 1950s he became very nearly the Prophet of the Western World, though some thought this more true in the provinces than in the home country. He became Britain's chief export to the United States, A. J. P. Taylor sneered; at one point he seemed to have taken over the *New York Times Magazine*; he was invited to Australia for lectures. He poured out articles, books, lectures. In regard to the mounting body of commentary on his main work, where it seemed that no historian's bibliography was regarded as complete without an article criticizing Toynbee, there was a tendency to reject all his conclusions yet regard him as still, somehow, a giant. The formidable philosopher-historian R. G. Collingwood condemned his whole procedure as erroneous yet pointed out that in practice Toynbee surmounted the limitations of his theory to write superb history.[2] Hans Kohn had declared that even while disagreeing with him historians "will be indebted to Dr. Toynbee for a provocative inspiration to think again, and to think out of a deeper knowledge."[3] Richard Chase suggested that "great and persuasive theorists—Marx, Freud, Toynbee—do not . . . exert their strongest influence because of the logical air-tightness of their theories, but rather because they fill an unconsciously felt vacuum with the force and urgency of their moral passion,"[4] The philosopher James Feibleman held, with others, that Toynbee had "made a start at least in the direction of a science of society," even if he had not finished it.[5] Most remarkable of all, H. Stuart Hughes of Harvard regretted, upon the publication of *Reconsiderations* in 1961, that Toynbee had replied to his critics at all, on the grounds that the *Study of History* should be left standing intact, warts and all, as a kind of monument to the vigor and weakness of the human mind.[6]

What most of the above seemed to be saying was that

Toynbee's significance, and his grandeur, transcend the various criticisms that may be made of him in detail; that, though the latter are numerous and damning, the former may remain untarnished. The merits of the work as a whole overcome its many partial defects.[7] The men of science, Samuel Butler had once observed, tell a lot of little truths for one big lie; the men of religion tell a lot of little lies for one big truth. Perhaps that is what Toynbee's defenders often meant. If so, it should be taken under advisement. This view, curiously enough, seems directly countered by another one frequently offered: that it is in the parts rather than the whole that Toynbee is best (which is what Collingwood went on to say in the passage cited above); that the system is worthless but the digressions magnificent. So stern a critic as Pieter Geyl found Toynbee in detail "striking and original . . . sometimes illuminating . . . neither a dull nor insignificant writer"; his quarrel was chiefly with the system (Geyl, *Debates with Historians*, pp. 176–77). And, of course, there remained those who took the simple view that, the foundations being faulty, no sound structure could be reared upon them. "Unless his history is scrupulous and consistent," it cannot be worth anything.[8]

All these avenues need to be explored, and it will be seen that many perplexing issues are raised. Some have praised Toynbee for a scientific approach to history, others because he put down the scientists and dared to affirm the dignity of a spiritual dimension. Some condemned him because he tried to reduce history to quasi-scientific laws, and others because he was a mystic and an irrationalist. Some thought of him as primarily an artist, others held that his prolix and barbarous prose impeded acceptance of his message. What is unquestionably true is that a vigorous debate was stimulated — vigorous and far-reaching. The publication of several books of collected essays on Toynbee [9] scarcely scratched the surface of the literature, which is still going on and of which the mastery must escape all but the Toynbee specialist (which the author of the following *tour d'horizon* cannot claim to be).

Fortunately for the student of Toynbee he himself, with characteristic energy, produced an enormous book dealing with his critics, and thus became the leading authority on himself. It stands as a performance hard to match in all the annals of literature. Since time immemorial angry authors have struck back at critics; but has any author ever before patiently collected and set forth all of the many hundreds of things that had been written against him? In so doing Toynbee surprised at least one of his most persistent gadflies, the Dutch historian Pieter Geyl, who had declared that Toynbee would never answer his critics, because he could not.[10] *Reconsiderations* (1961), which stands as volume 12 of *A Study of History* (vol. 11 having consisted of maps and gazeteer), was Toynbee's riposte, and it revealed him as a man of seeming humility and a remarkably objective lover of truth. *Time* magazine called it "an astonishing admission of error." It is not clear why it should be astonishing for a scholar working as pioneer in a vast and dimly lighted domain to admit error; as Toynbee observed, he had never posited his own infallibility or omniscience.[11] But perceptive readers noted that Toynbee repelled all major assaults on his empire. He adjusted his classification of civilizations, but kept his criteria and remained convinced that civilizations *can* be classified according to these criteria. He defended his method of comparative history, and his use of myth and metaphor as tools, as stoutly as he clung to his conclusions about the role of religion in human destiny. He denied that he was a prophet, but renewed his prophecies. But he rendered a service in gathering up a tremendous number of the criticisms leveled against his work.

Among significant revisions of his earlier views in *Reconsiderations* was a substantial modification of the classification of civilizations. The six primary civilizations became seven, Indic being separated from its earlier relationship to Sumeric. A considerable number of "satellite civilizations," a wholly new category, swelled Toynbee's total of 19 or 21 or 22 to 27 or perhaps 30 (exact enumeration remained difficult). (He dropped the division of Chinese history into two civilizations but added a Vietnamese satellite. Several Andean and Middle American satellites were added, and Indic grew from one to four counting Tibetan and Southeast Asian satellites.) And relationships between civilizations grew more complex. Egyptiac, Sumeric, and Minoan families are no longer separate, isolated entities; it is allowed, for example, that the Syriac society had not one sire but three, receiving influences from Egypt and the Aegean (Minoan) as well as from Sumero-Akkadian, the new name for Sumeric. So also with Western, Orthodox Christian, and Arabic. A chart attempting to diagram this new system would show arrows running back and fourth between the families of civilizations, whereas this was not true of the original classification offered in volumes 1–6. Toynbee dropped his category of arrested civilizations, and seems also to have abandoned infra-affiliation as a type of descent. It would be hard to draw an exact diagram of the later system. One feels that Toynbee is on the road to giving up the simple lines of the original and perhaps, therefore, the whole concept of separate and identifiable civilizations as units of scientific study, though he does attempt to save it as far as possible.

Though mostly on minor matters, the list of concessions made to criticism in *Reconsiderations* is admittedly a long one. But in many cases Toynbee pointed reasonably enough to new evidence that had come to light in the several decades since he began his *Study*. The considerable revision of the classification of civilizations is based on such evidence, from archeological discoveries in China, the New World, the Near East, which is discussed at length in *Reconsiderations*. Toynbee also conceded that he "exaggerated" or "put too much weight on" such motifs as withdrawal-and-return (pp. 264–65), the contrast between ruling and dominant minorities, original creation versus mimesis. Civilizations are less unique than he intimated, there is more interaction and diffusion (pp. 345 ff.). The leap from primitive society to civilization was less sudden than he thought (evidence from Jericho expeditions adduced, pp. 317–19). He gave ground on any number of other points. This is a softening of the sharply etched lines of the original, and may be why Stuart Hughes regretted the whole reply: the *Study*, right or wrong, has an architectural grandeur which is blurred by such concessions. Still, on the whole Toynbee did not retract, but pleaded the inevitable oversimplification of a beginning hypothesis. One is bound to wonder, in this regard, whether if enough scholarship is brought to bear on hypotheses they are altogether overthrown, and we are back to H. A. L. Fisher's planless confusion of things. Imagination constructs a pattern, fact overthrows it. But Toynbee conceded only that his generalizations must be refined, not abandoned.

It would seem, then, that criticisms of Toynbee's view of history might be sorted out as errors of fact; apparent errors of historical interpretation; and several questions about his conception of history and historical method. Beyond this there are questions about his treatment of religion and theology, and objections to his political ideology and values. In addition to the matter of literary style, there remains the question of whether the work as a whole, as vision or as art, rises above the various criticisms of its parts. Though imperfect, this outline may perhaps serve as a workable plan for a relatively concise discussion of the great Toynbee debate.

Errors of Fact and Interpretation

Some purported to see in Toynbee a man remarkably careless of his facts. A few samples may be given. In an early review of the *Study of History*, Charles A. Beard stood appalled at the ignorance that made Woodrow Wilson a North Carolinian.[12] It may be observed that Toynbee's slips become peculiarly important because they are normally used to support some law or generalization. An average creaturely historian might have called Wilson a North Carolinian *en passant* without a major case being made of it, but Toynbee in volume 4 uses this as an example of "the nemesis of creativity," one of his chief patterns of breakdown, illustrating how "idolization of a once glorious past" handicapped the post-Civil War South, North Carolina escaping this curse because it had not played a leading part in the antebellum glory. When he corrected this blunder, Toynbee substituted the name of another North Carolinian, not nearly so eminent as President Wilson, evidently indicating that once he had made up his mind to use this glittering theory, he could as well find evidence in one place as another. It would have been just as easy to find equally eminent *South* Carolinians, we are likely to think. At any rate Toynbee while removing Wilson's name did not change the generalization. We have drifted into the question of Toynbee's method, but it is closely connected with his use of factual evidence, the point being that Toynbee's factual evidence presumably provides the empirical basis for "laws" or typical patterns of behavior. Those who charge that Toynbee refuses to modify or reject his laws in the light of the evidence might point to such a case as the above.

But such cases are not numerous. There were numerous minor errors, such as Toynbee corrected in his errata (see, for example, vol. 10, p. vii, 1954 printing), which seem of no great account. (The magnitude of his subject makes errors of this sort inevitable.) Then there is the type of apparent error that may really belong in other categories, being a matter of interpretation, or perhaps of methodological assumptions, but which clearly involves factual evidence. If Toynbee (as Pieter

Geyl was utterly dismayed to learn) thinks that England cut herself off from European affairs from 1588 on for several centuries (an example of withdrawal-and-return), his forgetfulness of the wars of Louis XIV and other matters may be an example of historical ignorance, and Toynbee partly admitted the truth of the charge in *Reconsiderations* (pp. 265–66). But he insisted that his interpretation was nevertheless in some sense true, and perhaps it was. There are many patterns in history. To what extent is Toynbee behaving illegitimately when he selects his evidence to prove a thesis? It is a question better left for later treatment. But clearly an historian cannot properly ignore matters of fact which are plainly present and which disprove his thesis, without at least explaining himself.[13]

It is often hard to decide whether Toynbee is factually wrong or merely adopting a possible interpretation. His staggering erudition is matched at times by an almost equally astonishing innocence. To relate Rousseau to "Archaism" (6, p. 58; 9, p. 463) by identifying him with a back to nature or primitivist position is to commit an elementary textbook misconstrual of Jean-Jacques, long since exploded, though still popularly believed. (For this view, Toynbee cites only Oswald Spengler!) The same may be said for the assumption that science and religion have been locked in mortal conflict since the time of Galileo (7, pp. 465–83). Romanticism is also identified as an archaism (8, pp. 132, 135) but the fact that the Romantics found inspiration in aspects of the Middle Ages does not mean that theirs was not a fresh spiritual attitude for Europe. We have previously commented on the same mistake in reference to the Renaissance. A significant point is that Toynbee seldom argues these interpretations; he simply takes them for granted, and uses them as support for one of the laws or patterns he is intent on illustrating. He needs ready-made historical illustrations and he takes these where he can find them, but often does not check to see whether they are or are not true. Thus he is constantly at the mercy of secondhand authorities and even of his unverified prejudices.

Possibly the most bizarre outgrowth of Toynbee's a priori dogmatism, imposing itself on his interpretation of history, is his rejection of borrowing from a prior age. This has been alluded to in connection with the section on Renaissances. He attempts to separate what is indigenous (good, creative) from what is taken from a "dead" past, which is uncreative, doomed, "necromantic." The interpretations that flow from this dictum are simply grotesque. For example (9, p. 166), we learn that Thomas Aquinas revealed his genius "not in the resuscitation of Aristotelian theses but in the construction of a system that was the Angelic Doctor's own." That Aquinas created something that was his own would be widely conceded; that he used Aristotle to this end is equally obvious. It is false—and very strange in an historian—to attempt in this way to separate the past materials on which a thinker (or a culture) operates, from his "own" achievement. All creative work involves absorbing the previous intellectual heritage and then going on from there. As Acton put it, "The strongest minds are those that have known how to avail themselves most effectively of previous ideas." For Aquinas and the medieval European mind, Greek philosophy was a necessary starting place. There is not one part of Aquinas's *Summa Theologica*—to put it another way—which is imitative Aristotelianism, and another part which is indigenous Aquinas; the work as a whole is saturated with Aristotle but reveals originality in its application of Aristotle to Christian problems. There is something wrong with an historian who cannot see so obvious a fact; and the something that is wrong, obviously, is one or more predetermined positions which are inserted into the history from outside in a wholly arbitrary manner. Toynbee has decided that Hellenism was another civilization, so its thought must be alien and unhealthy for the West. He has decided that the "pagan" elements which he dislikes in modern civilization came from Hellas, and he would like to discard them. What he has *not* done is to look at Aquinas and his age from within, from their own standpoint, and understand them as they were. (Toynbee appears to have no real knowledge of Aquinas and cites for this construal, which so conveniently fits his thesis, an obsolete textbook.)

Such questions could be extended almost ad infinitum, for they spring to mind on every page of Toynbee. The above examples are taken from European history, since this writer's competence, such as it is, extends little further; but of course the real impressiveness of the *Study* lies in its simultaneous excursions into Russia, China, India, Islam, Persia, and other exotic realms. But it appears that students in these areas have the same criticisms. The following are examples:

1] Geoffrey Barraclough has remarked that "The verdict of every competent authority on East Europe" is that "Dr. Toynbee's interpretation of Russian history is arbitrary and unacceptable," [14] and a number of articles have been written on this subject. [15]

2] Students of China have seemingly found Toynbee's ideas about Chinese history almost too absurd to discuss. Raymond Dawson has spoken of "misconceptions on a monumental scale, which would never be accepted, let alone suggested, by any Sinologist," which are not wholly rectified by his abandonment in *Reconsiderations* of the two-civilization theory, and which suggest a ruthless forcing of Chinese data into his preconceptions. [16] The Chinese historians have convicted Toynbee of flat error in regard to the physical features of the Yellow River valley, used as an example of the challenge of an adverse environment affecting the rise of civilization. They find his view of the Han period as a time of decay fantastic, though doubtless no more fantastic than the parallel conception of medieval Byzantium and Renaissance Europe as periods of breakdown. And they find numerous other errors. The verdict would apparently have to be that in applying his model of the rise, growth, and decline of civilization to China, Toynbee relied upon an imposing ignorance of the facts. Here, to be sure, he has been the victim of a considerable rise in knowledge of Chinese history in recent years.

Other criticisms from area specialists are almost too numerous to mention.[17] They are by no means always devoid of respect and praise for Toynbee. Islamists who cannot accept his classifications (a "contrived stylization of historical fact") can praise him for calling attention to the unity of Islamic civilization.[18] Historians of India are not completely hostile.[19]

The indignant uprising of the Jews against Toynbee may be less historical than religious and political, or perhaps based on misunderstandings. The furious Jewish attack, expressed in such works as Maurice Samuel's *The Professor and the Fossil* (1956), and Abba Eban's *The Toynbee Heresy* (1955), was in part a result of Toynbee calling Jewish civilization a "fossil," by which he meant no more than that it had survived the larger society of which it had originally been a part (an unfortunate and also not very accurate term, as he conceded in *Reconsiderations*). He also singled out Zionism as an example of opprobrious nationalism, and many times criticized the present state of Israel for its treatment of the Arabs. In volumes 2 and 3 the Jew serves as an example of the stimulus of adversity, in a successful response for which however the Jews paid a price in a distortion of their nature. Toynbee associates the Judaic element in Christianity with the narrow intolerance of the "Jealous God" (6, pp. 38–49; 7, p. 439, etc.). It could hardly escape notice that to Toynbee Christianity is a higher and superior religion than Judaism; in volume 4, for example, the nemesis of creativity overtakes the Jews in that, infatuated with their monotheistic achievement in the past, they cannot advance to accept Christianity. That he felt enormous respect for the Judaic tradition and regarded Zionism as a betrayal of true Judaism, a proposition with which many pious Jews would agree, did little to dampen the fires, and a considerable shelf might be filled with Jewish attacks on Toynbee. But this is conceivably because the Jews are both a thin-skinned and an articulate people.[20] In *Avenues of History* (1952), Sir Lewis Namier conceded that "to my knowledge no anti-Jewish feeling ever entered into" Toynbee's anti-Zionism, which he attributed to his pro-Islamic position reaching back to 1919. One might attribute it to his antinationalism, and to his expecting more from the Jews than a repetition of the ways of power politics and racial intolerance.

The underlying criticism of Toynbee is that he forces the facts to fit his theory. This is a question of method, and can be discussed under that heading. It issues in evident errors of fact and interpretation because Toynbee does not seek open-mindedly to ascertain the historical reality—to discover what Aquinas and Rousseau and Marx and Mussolini did in fact feel and think. He does not take them in the context of their time. He grabs on to possible construals of their work—as often as not using secondhand evidence and forced interpretations—because these fit his formulae. If you want to know anything about the above worthies, it is no good going to Toynbee; you will only discover something about *him*. Obviously this is not true of all of Toynbee but this is because he frequently abandons his "system" to write straightforward history. He does this on subjects which he knows firsthand, and such passages are often splendid. The digressive passages of straight history are what swell *A Study of History* to ten massive volumes when, as many have pointed out, its bulk could be reduced substantially so far as concerns the structural system (as in fact D. C. Somervell did reduce it). But if he had treated all his subjects as he treats a few, the total bulk would have been a hundred volumes, not ten. What we get are occasional lapses into straight history incongruously married to a dogmatic theoretical structure that is not history at all.

Perhaps a certain habitual carelessness toward facts may be alleged as the natural accompaniment of a mind

as imaginative and fertile in hypotheses as Toynbee's. It
may be observed in other writings. For example, in his
recent, 1967, *Acquaintances*, he tells the story of Woodrow Wilson's aloofness aboard the *George Washington*
en route to the Peace Conference in late 1918. The story
has often been told, by just about everyone who was on
that ship. They all record that Wilson did at length
emerge from what seemed his haughty seclusion to address the members of the "Inquiry" and others of the
humbler workers in the American delegation. As Toynbee recalls hearing it from W. L. Westermann, Wilson
never did emerge, but remained in his stateroom from
beginning to end of the voyage (p. 201). Toynbee is
certainly wrong here, for many witnesses have recorded
the very words of the president on the occasion of his
emergence; [21] and the mistake must surely be Toynbee's
not Westermann's, who would certainly have known of
the occasion in question. Perhaps one should not make
much of an old man's lapse of memory many years after
the event; on the other hand the Toynbee of *Acquaintances* is far from senile, the event was a reasonably famous one, and Toynbee uses it in a context of
discrediting the whole Peace Conference which, as we
have noted, was a severe disenchantment for him. Does
Toynbee frequently allow his bias and his ordering
imagination subtly to distort the substance of events?
The charge has frequently been made. We are reminded
of Mark Twain's observation that nothing in history
ever happens exactly as it should have—the historian
corrects this defect. What a corrector of history's dis-
order is Toynbee!

Toynbee's Scientific Laws

Events must be made to fit the pattern. Such is
the burden of everyone's criticism, so that it becomes
virtually the only issue among historians: "His in-

sistence on pigeonholing and labelling everything in history to make it fit one way or another into the over-rationalized patterns he seeks to find (or impose?)." [22] From every side the specialist historians, writing what Herbert Butterfield has called "technical history," turned thumbs down on Toynbee. But he in turn has rejected their kind of history, sometimes because it seems to him too narrow, too parochial; sometimes because he is apparently impervious to the kind of "understanding" that is the reward of the history that seeks, as the "science of the particular," to expose the unique inwardness of a situation; [23] but mostly because he is seeking generalizations or laws, on the basis of a comparison of societies and processes.

In *Reconsiderations* Toynbee stoutly defended the attempt to find general laws, [24] along with his method for finding them. Though in fact he had done so all along, it was rather startling to some that Toynbee insisted upon his being nothing more than a humble laborer in the vineyard of science. He affected embarrassed surprise at being called prophet or poet; nothing of that at all. His huge system, with its apocalyptic religious overtones, turns out to be nothing more (or less), in the eye of its creator, than an honest attempt to advance the science of history, the goal of which is to discover general laws or "regularities," and then, presumably, to use them to predict and control (cf. p. 327: the "intellectual profits" which will follow from a correct apprehension of the laws of history).

So far as concerns history and probably all the social sciences, Toynbee's program went against the grain of thought in this century. The total Science of Man dreamed of by eighteenth-century *philosophes* such as Montesquieu and Condorcet, and reaffirmed by early nineteenth-century Positivists such as Comte and Buckle, had appeared to fail badly in the hands of such would-be practitioners as Marx and Spencer. (Perhaps they succeeded as prophets, but not as scientists.) The chief reason was that the empirical data stubbornly refused to conform to any of the grand schemes suggested. By selective use of evidence data could be made to conform to any number; but Clio thus violated always exacted her revenge by disclosing data which the generalizer had concealed. Of Marx's essentially a priori or speculative history, a distinguished scholar (J. H. Hexter) has remarked (in accents which virtually all competent historians would approve) that it can be held only by resolutely ignoring three-quarters of the past and asking no very bright questions about the rest. History can be depicted as the story of progress, or of decay, or of ever-recurring cycles; as controlled by economic forces, or political forces, or intellectual forces; as a story of heroism and courage, or of cruelty and cowardice; of class war or mutual cooperation; and so on. Which is right? All, and none. We know enough to construct many interpretations of the past, but we do not know enough to choose among them.

The growing scepticism about historical "laws" received assistance from historians and philosophers of post-Positivist Europe, in the age of Nietzsche, Dilthey, Croce, Bergson. It was Toynbee's own generation, since he grew to intellectual maturity in the 1900s; but it was mostly a European as distinct from a British moment, though some Anglo-Americans were deeply influenced by it and Toynbee might have learned much, later, from R. G. Collingwood. Broadly speaking it was the view of this group that history had been harmed by a misguided effort to harness her to the chariot of physical science, falsely conceiving it to be her function to establish isolated "facts," and then use these facts to build up "laws" of an ever-increasing level of generalization. It does not follow that the only alternative to this is a conception of history as merely a branch of fancy letters. History is an autonomous study, and a science in its way, but the science of the *particular*. Its goal is to intuit and recreate past action, from the "inside," in all its uniqueness. This is done with the aid of the historical imagination, as well as the critical intelligence.

This sort of understanding, if it is of an important problem or process, is self-rewarding, and it is of aid to us in the present because it enables us to know the origins of our situation. History does not provide us with any ready-made solutions, but it enables us more fully to understand ourselves and our age. Our situation is unique, and will never be repeated. History never "repeats itself," there cannot be "historical laws." Such an explanation corresponds rather well with most practicing historians' feeling of what they are in fact doing. Most historians strive to reproduce some significant past episode in all its uniqueness and concreteness, and feel they have succeeded if they can do this, and also show how it affected the present.

In seeking to embrace the whole of humanity in one great framework of law, Toynbee was actually quite an old-fashioned historian. He had not kept up with the advance of theory and philosophy of history which, since Wilhelm Dilthey and others at the end of the nineteenth century, had been going in quite different directions. This most important and most distinguished line of recent thinking about the nature of the historian's work rejected and disproved the older, nineteenth-century vision of a single, knowable, finite body of historical data, which some day would be completed and would disclose *the* past, probably as a single structure of law or orderly development. It has taught us that there are many pasts—in fact an infinite number; that what we think of as "past" is something that changes with each new experience, bringing a new perspective; that these views of the past are never finished and are subject to constant reinterpretation. The new theorists of history have also stressed—and, in the case of Karl Popper, claimed to have proved—the unpredictability of the future. In R. G. Collingwood's words, "The historian who tries to forecast the future is like a tracker anxiously peering at a muddy road in order to descry the footsteps of the next person who is going to pass that way." Toynbee does, of course, like the old historiosophers claim to be able to forecast the future in major ways ("The Future World Order," etc.).

Toynbee's outlook seems quaint and naïve to this twentieth-century school, which has blended with much more sophisticated, and less optimistic, strands of modernism. Reinhold Niebuhr—to take one example—writing in roughly the same generation as Toynbee, smiled at the innocence of those who entertained the illusion that human problems can be disposed of by social science quite as efficiently as technology can handle physical ones. In *The Irony of American History* (1952) he says

> the whole drama of history is enacted in a frame of meaning too large for human comprehension or management. It is a drama in which fragmentary meanings can be discerned within a penumbra of mystery; and in which specific duties and responsibilities can be undertaken within a vast web of relations which are beyond our powers. (P. 88)

Such resigned pessimism is the fruit of a wisdom deeper than Toynbee's, no doubt. It was not in his essentially Victorian mind to accept it. He never understood that the task begun by Ibn Khaldun and carried on by Montesquieu could not be completed at last.

More recently, neopositivists such as Karl Popper and Carl Hempel have tried to save history for something more nearly "scientific" than the frankly intuitive and imaginative procedures of the Croce-Collingwood school by agreeing that history seeks the explanation of particular situations but arguing that it does so by *applying* general laws. Most other sciences use particulars to arrive at generalizations; history (like geology) uses generalizations to explain particulars. But these neopositivists agree that history has no predictive functions and indeed Popper has been most severe with those who have claimed to discover "inexorable laws of historical destiny"—a delusion that has done more damage to mankind than any other sort of thinking.[25] This would seem to leave Toynbee isolated, and in accounts of historical theory he is indeed singled out as apparently occupying a lonely position—"apparently," because many are not convinced that he consistently does so.[26]

Anthropologists and sociologists have likewise, it appears, concluded against grand historical generalizations. Raymond Aron in his recent survey of sociology asks, "Is the time of 'the great doctrines of historical sociology' definitely past?" and seems to suggest an affirmative answer.[27] The reaction against simplistic schemes of evolutionary development such as Spencer's pushed anthropology far toward the opposite extreme of studying cultures as they are, for their own sake, without attempting to posit any evolutionary order or hierarchy.[28] Micro-sociology has replaced macro-sociology, leaving such a large figure as P. Sorokin isolated, viewed as a splendid anachronism by most of his professional colleagues.[29] Such at any rate was the dominating trend through the first half of the century.

The preceding digression helps explain the severely negative reaction to Toynbee's innocent claim to be ferreting out laws of historical development on the largest possible scale. His critics tend to be divided between those who think that no historical or sociological laws at all are possible and those who think that they are possible only on a far more modest scale.[30] They agree that *A Study of History* quite fails in its purpose though they may see it alternatively as a throwback to older Positivist modes or as a pioneer study breaking ground for a future scientific history. (Some of those who contrast the mere empiricism of old-fashioned history, narrative or unguided, with up-to-date scientific horizons seem strangely ignorant of the Croce-Collingwood line of thought, which is really much more up-to-date than scientism, now several centuries old.)

Against this barrage of criticism of his basic methodology and conception of history, what is Toynbee's defense? Sometimes it seems weak. He says that at least his system is not as bad as Marx's (12, p. 141, n); and he has always posited a human *need* for "a comprehensive view of human affairs"—yet he has also detected error in this "will-o'-the-wisp of omniscience," a form of arrogance and idolatry (10, pp. 24–41). That a felt need exists seems hardly a good argument for a science; we would think it strange if a physicist should support or reject a theory on such grounds, arguing, for instance, that indeterminacy cannot be true because men like to think in deterministic patterns. If this need is his defense, has not Toynbee implicitly abandoned his allegedly scientific orientation in order to cater to quite unscientific desires? This felt need for a total view of human history is a quasi-religious urge, prophetic and emotional. It may well be that Toynbee is justified in responding to it; but that is to place the valuation of his work on another plane. It is inconsistent with his claim to be purely a scientist.

The proof of the pudding is in the eating, and so we should glance at the "laws" which Toynbee does in fact discover. Digressively, it may be noted that historians anxious to place themselves on the side of science have in the past alleged rather dubious laws. Rising in 1923 to address the American Historical Association, veteran historian Edward P. Cheyney talked about "Law in History" and declared among other things that

> The continuity of history is not merely a fact, it is a law. . . . There seems to be a law of impermanence, or mutability. . . . There seems to be a law of interdependence . . . of individuals, of classes, of tribes, of nations. . . . There seems to be a law of democracy, a tendency for all governments to come under the control of the people. . . . There seems to be a law of moral progress. . . . These are laws to be reckoned with much as are the laws of gravitation or of chemical affinity, or of organic evolution, or of human psychology.[31]

It will be noted by the least critical that some of these laws are so vague as to be useless: what would we think of a chemist who announced that he had discovered the law that things tend to change? Others represent trends or directions in certain areas and periods of time: even if it was true that democracy was on the increase in 1923 (just after Mussolini took over Italy and just before Stalin began to take over Russia), we could not have been sure that this trend would continue, nor had it always been a trend in all places in the past. Still others are only partly true, if at all: if there is interdependence, there is also conflict, wherein Karl Marx and others have seen a great "law" of history. A law of this sort is rather like a chemist stating that *sometimes* molecules blend with each other. None of Cheyney's laws carry much conviction because altogether lacking in precision and certainty, and they are typical of the laws which historians used to claim to have discovered. Toynbee's are not different. Though some of them strike our imagination as powerful presentations of undeniably significant themes or motifs in human affairs, as "laws" they are either truisms, tautologies, temporary trends, or partial truths (analogies, Henri Marrou has suggested). And other "laws" of equal validity could be framed, which contradict Toynbee's.

Toynbee's main law of growth is hardly more than an assertion that change does in fact take place. An élan, a mysterious driving force impels men onward. His Yin-and-Yang effect may be the secret of the universe, for all we know, in some half-understood way. (Not only the wisdom of the Chinese but that of the ancient Greeks, beginning with Empedocles, posited alternating cycles of love and strife, rest and dynamism.) The latest speculations of astrophysics suggest an immense and ultimate rhythm of one primeval atom, exploding and sending matter and energy outward for eighty billion years, following which comes a long contraction and then presumably another explosion. But such speculations about the cosmic cycle, even if proven, are not what science means by "laws." The proof, if any, of the cosmic process just referred to lies in the application of

innumerable more precise laws of the behavior of matter
and energy. In any case such speculations about human
history are only that. Concretely, Toynbee only posits
that there is change, and there is human creativity,
which responds to the challenge of change.

Toynbee's critics have had a field day with Challenge
and Response, since it seems so tautological.[32] A creative
challenge is by definition what man can answer with a
response. That the challenge may be too great, or
not great enough, or just right, is Toynbee's "law,"
which seems to resemble Goldilocks'. (Actually it would
be reasonable to suppose that at any time there is an
almost infinite number of challenges of finely graduated
degrees of difficulty.) Toynbee offers us no real criteria
for deciding when or why challenges will be met. He
provides us with examples, to be sure. And he com-
plains, in *Reconsiderations*, that some tax him with
giving insufficient evidence for his laws while others
accuse him of overwhelming them with too many examples. This is not an inconsistency in his critics, as he
suggests. A chemist who proposed the hypothesis that
things do change could then cite examples without end
—and without meaningful order. Toynbee's law of
Challenge and Response is too broad and vague. It resembles the Ten Commandments and the Rights of
Man in having a moral but hardly a scientific significance. That Toynbee leaves his laws so vague, and
that he provides us with no specific dynamic of history
such as Marx alleges in the theory of historical materialism (a point often noticed),[33] may be to his credit
as historian, for he recognizes both the complex multi-
causality of social phenomena and the always elusive
"x-factor" in human reactions, but it is an implicit
abandonment of the scientific claim.

Toynbee's other laws can be subjected to the same
sort of destructive criticism endlessly. It may be worth
giving one more example of a confused and partial law.
As we will recall, Toynbee asserts that during its breakdown and disintegration, institutions which once bred

life in a civilization now stifle it; virtues turn into vices; what worked once is now treated as a magic talisman, but times have changed and this clinging to the past leads to defeat. This "idolization of an ephemeral institution" or self is presented as an outstanding example of the "nemesis of creativity." That it often happens to individuals and to nations no one is likely to doubt. But is it a law of decay, occurring with regularity and certainty during periods of the decline of a civilization? Men are always learning the wrong lessons from history, but they do it as much in one stage as another. Sometimes they refrain from doing it. Sometimes they do it and it turns out to be the right thing. A good example would be the French clinging to Napoleon's mode of warfare in 1870 and Petain's in 1940; but the Germans meanwhile had creatively evolved a new and better mode.

In one of his leading examples of this, indeed the case on which he spends much the most space, Toynbee tells us that it was wrong of the Byzantines to cling to the Roman Empire; it was also wrong of Charlemagne and Otto the Great, but fortunately they were not able to achieve it. Both these cases occurred in the juvenile stages of a civilization in Toynbee's reckonings. The medieval East Roman Empire, according to Toynbee, was not the same at all as the old Roman Empire, which died with Justinian in 565; it was reborn as a new civilization in the eighth century with Leo Syrus, but apparently at its birth committed the mistake said to characterize old and dying civilizations. This is very odd. This separation of the Byzantine state into two parts is an example of Toynbee's arbitrary practices in identifying "civilizations," a point discussed in the next section. But in his view medieval Byzantine was a new civilization as was the medieval West at the same time. Most historians think that it was not wrong of these societies to seek to restore the Roman state, which was far superior in its concepts of law and government to anything the barbarian Germans knew. But, if we accept

Toynbee's classification of civilizations and if we agree that this was a case of blindly worshipping an old institution, it was still done in infancy, not in old age.

For the Byzantines it seemed to work quite well, since they went on to create a brilliant civilization under a large empire, which lasted at least three or four centuries. For Western Europe, it was, according to Toynbee, a blessing in disguise that she did not achieve a similar leviathan state marked by caesaro-papism, which would have blighted the Papacy. Charlemagne seems never to have aimed at a caesaro-papism; but apart from that, we have here a principle of nemesis which sometimes works out well when one tries to adopt it and does not succeed. We feel extremely confused. Among other queries, we feel inclined to ask what is the difference between following a usable tradition and being infatuated with the past; and what is meant by "nemesis"? (If it takes three hundred or four hundred years to take effect, was the disaster not perhaps due to something else?) Questions of causation arise, always terribly difficult ones in history: can we be sure that Europe flourished because Charlemagne failed, and can we be sure that Byzantium fell, belatedly, because she revived the Roman Empire? (Toynbee's causal assumptions are very frequently breathtaking.)

In the end we will probably conclude, as before, that an interpretation for which a plausible case can sometimes be made in a specific situation has been stretched beyond all clear and verifiable meaning, indeed beyond the widest boundaries of credibility. Science insists that its laws be verifiable. Experiment is never open to the historian as it is to the physical scientist; but evidence can be presented for the view, say, that the French in 1939 were victimized by memories of 1917, or the British in 1956 by memories of 1936–39. Such evidence might convince us that the "Munich reflex" was one factor, if not the only one, in determining Anthony Eden to strike at Egypt. It is difficult to see what evidence could be presented to verify the proposition that

Constantinople fell in 1453 because Leo Syrus did not establish an independent church in the eighth century. (The evidence that Toynbee does present has been challenged by Byzantine experts.) [34] A useful principle of interpretation has been inflated into a law of vast dimensions, and as such it is a pseudo law.

After all, the giveaway on Toynbee's claim to be nothing but a humble scientist, content with empirical methods, is the all-encompassing scope of his project. A scientist would surely have begun on a simpler level. Toynbee speaks of the enormous difficulties in the area of inquiry he has chosen; it would seem, then, natural not to begin by trying to do the whole job at once. The sciences are full of just such abortive efforts, in the infancy of the science, to do too much. "The worst error in the early stages is to expect to arrive at a complete view, to formulate a theory which is of universal application and is going to be the last word," as A. D. Ritchie, a writer on scientific methods, has observed. Whether or not it will ever be possible, a study like Toynbee's, essaying nothing less than the final answer to the rhythm of all history, cannot be written yet, for humbler historians have hardly begun to do the foundation work. From a Toynbeean point of view, little of what is done as historical research today is of much use; we must have comparative history, not the study of unique situations. Comparative history, seeking to discover more specific laws or trends, can be applied on the level of specific problems, such as Ronald Syme and Rupert Wilkinson have tried to do for governing elites, Crane Brinton and others for "the anatomy of revolution," and Karl Wittfogel for types of despotism. This is perhaps what Toynbee should have been doing, and would have done were he not a romantic and prophetic writer utterly different in temperament from the scientist. Like Marx, he has borrowed the costume of the scientists but fitted it to his religio-ethical purposes.

It would be quite wrong, though, to suggest that Toynbee's inventive formulations have no value. If only he did not overdo it! (He has confessed to a fatal tendency to "go too far.") His laws, if taken as local patterns, do, for the most part, correspond to basic human processes, such as other sociologists and historians and artists have observed. They intriguingly resemble psychological processes as well. The change from creative response to mimesis, which Toynbee sees as a phenomenon of decline, and which is matched by a change in the elite from a creative to a merely dominant minority, resembles Max Weber's contrast between charisma and bureaucracy, or Robert Michels's "iron law of oligarchy," or, again, Weber's and Pareto's "disenchantment" process: the initial spontaneous phase of a movement hardens into bureaucratic routine, institutionalization sets in at the expense of humanization. The foxes take over from the lions, in Vilfredo Pareto's metaphor. Others than Toynbee apply it on a smaller scale; it is happening all the time. It happened to the German Socialist party between 1880 and 1910, as Michels described in his famous work on *Political Parties*. It has happened to the Soviet Union from the exalted apocalyptic mood of the "ten days that shook the world" in 1917 through the cruel but still personal despotism of Stalin to the bureaucratic age of Brezhnev. In the history of the Church, waves of personalism and even antinomianism have come periodically to batter against institutional formalism, only to ossify and become targets for the next generation of protestants. Mankind is always fighting the battle to keep alive its enthusiasms and to organize them without destroying them. Everything begins in *mystique* and ends in *politique* (Péguy).

The complaint against Toynbee's use of this motif is that he seldom applies it precisely enough. It floats vaguely over whole civilizations. It is applied indiscriminantly to entire epochs, and entire societies. As applied to the Hellenic-Roman civilization (always Toynbee's main model), we are apparently asked to contrast the leaders of Athens in its golden age with the Roman emperors: the former ruling by charm, the latter by force. But surely there is no one continuous sociological process here. The process of decline or disenchantment was at work within the Attic state, as it was within Rome: from Augustus and Marcus Aurelius to the later emperors, perhaps. Charisma and creativity, indeed, can and do appear at any time. Toynbee derives these patterns from correctly observing human behavior as it appears in individuals and in groups; then he applies them sweepingly to epochs of history. The error would seem to lie partly in personifying or anthropomorphizing epochs and civilizations, making them like individuals: essentially the same organic fallacy committed by Oswald Spengler.

Other Toynbee motifs are subject to similar objections. That it does sometimes help in the creative process to "withdraw" for a time (see Graham Wallas, *The Art of Thought* [1926]), and that men and groups obviously suffer sometimes from the intoxication of victory, called more simply overconfidence, does not mean that these are laws determining the rise and fall of civilizations. "Schism," both "in the soul" and "in the body social," does indeed seem to be a phenomenon of decline and fall. It has been noticed by Durkheim and other sociologists as the "anomie" that results from "dysfunction," when "solidarity" is replaced by an anarchic individualism, and

> *Things fall apart, the centre cannot hold,*
> *Mere anarchy is loosed upon the world.*
> (YEATS, "The Second Coming")

Or, as the alienation of the artist and intellectual from his society. That we live in an "age of anxiety" (Koestler, Baumer, Jaspers) is the result of this loss of social integration or community in modern industrial society, which puts individuals on their own, without the aid of accepted social authority and acknowledged religious beliefs, in a complex and confusing world. No doubt something similar happened in the latter stages of the

Roman Empire. The Hellenistic phase of ancient culture—cosmopolitan, vulgar, scientific, groping for faith
—has seemed to many an historian to bear comparison
with our own.[35] Toynbee's examination of social disintegration is suggestive; but it would require much
sharper analysis and fullness of statement to be meaningful. His attempt to chart a topology of the soul by
throwing all of thought and feeling into a few large
piles is breathtaking in its naïveté. Are we all either
transfigured or detached?

The Comparative Method and the
Classification of Civilizations

If we reduce Toynbee's inflated claims to be
discovering laws or regularities applicable to each civilization, we may agree that he is writing comparative
history and that this is worth doing. On this it may
first be said that though he has rarely carried them out,
Toynbee has suggested many interesting projects. There
seems every reason to accept the method of comparative
history, even if we decide that it can lead to few ab-
solutely valid generalizations. It is one of the ways historians can illuminate human affairs. It is not the only
way, and for some it is not the most fruitful way, but it
surely is a legitimate way. Faced with some striking
event—a revolution, war, migration, riot—(which normally touches off all inquiry), the historian can approach it in several different ways, seeking explanation
and understanding. He can offer a full description, bringing to light all the factors, those hidden as well as those
superficially known—getting at the complete story, as
nearly as possible, of who, when, where, what. He can
strive for a re-creation from within, seeking by historical
imagination to get inside the minds of the actors to
discover their motives, their thought-processes. Most
historians do both of the above, mingling description

with motive-analysis and bringing to bear literary skill to evoke a vivid picture of men in action in a complex situation. But the historian may also show the event as part of a larger pattern, and if he is a good historian he will certainly do some of this. He can do so by revealing the event's relationship to other events, past or contemporary. He will show us how the Russian Revolution touched both the Russian past, the European Socialist movement, the climate of ideas, the war, the economic situation, and other things. He takes it out of isolation and puts it in the context of much larger and longer processes.

But he can also choose to show the event in comparison with other events of the same sort: compare the Russian Revolution with other revolutions, pointing out similarities and differences, discovering common denominators. There are dangers and limitations in this procedure, but so there are in the others. There is no reason why this avenue should not be explored. In its behalf it may be said that this approach is interesting and exciting, and does produce knowledge that stimulates and illuminates. There is no reason for confining it, Toynbee-wise, to a comparison of civilizations. One can fruitfully compare international situations, for example. Yet some of the intersocietal analogies suggested by Toynbee (but not at all thoroughly carried out by him) are exciting: for example, the comparison of Hinayana Buddhism, Stoicism, and modern Schopenhauerianism as ideologies of detachment, related to their social setting.

Comparative studies have recently experienced something of a boom (in literature, religion, government, as well as history). It is hard to judge how much Toynbee may have contributed to this, or how far he was a result of forces operating generally on the scholarly mind. The impulse came partly from increasing awareness of other peoples and cultures in a widening world. Writing in 1958 in the first issue of the journal *Comparative Studies in Society and History*, Professor Sylvia Thrupp stressed this theme: "we have acquired a sense of humanity." It is not clear, though, why one couldn't just learn about these new places without attempting to formalize something called "the comparative method." Some of the most admired examples of comparative history actually did not draw on exotic realms (e.g., Frank Tannenbaum's *Slave and Citizen*, comparing slavery in the United States and in Latin America). This approach found congenial quarters among some young historians who aspired to recover a scientific historiography with the aid of computers and more rigorous quantifying methods, and who also were interested in social, institutional subjects, such as slavery and revolutions and ruling classes, which lend themselves well to comparison. Like Toynbee, they sometimes looked toward the goal of a generalizing science able to provide useful prediction and control of significant social phenomena. They were impatient with traditional history which they regarded as descriptive, narrative, empirical, narrowly focused. Much of their work has been vitiated by muddled conceptualization, like Toynbee's: they insist on comparing things which are not really comparable, they are as naïve about human situations as they are sophisticated about statistical methods. Insofar as these historians pursued the old goal of exact laws on the model of the physical sciences (as a few did) they seem certain to fail. But comparison can stimulate the consideration of familiar subjects, by casting them in a new light, and it can yield interesting results in the area of causation, by discovering similar situations which had different antecedents. (Tannenbaum, in the book mentioned, asked the specific question why North American slavery died only after a violent war while South American expired peacefully, and thought he found an answer in the varying legal and cultural framework of Latin and Anglo-Saxon civilizations.)

Academically oriented, comparative studies usually took much more specific subjects than did Toynbee, and indeed it is the verdict of critical analysis that "comparison has been most useful in very restricted topical areas" (Paul K. Conkin). Nevertheless, Toynbee's general influence, and even his specific interest in comparing ruling classes, colonial elites, cultures in conflict has undoubtedly done much to stimulate the growth of research in such subjects. He is one of the founding fathers of comparison, even as he is of contacts between civilizations, and world history, as these have developed in our time.

But despite some interest in comparative history, historians continue mostly to write about the particular and the unique. There are surely more reasons for this than stale custom and lethargy. It may be more important, and useful, to note the uniqueness of things, rather than their similarities—even if we agree that there are similarities, as well as differences. It can be misleading to think of the likenesses rather than the differences. For example, Toynbee (2, p. 186 and elsewhere) lumps Leninist communism, Italian fascism, German nazism, and Mustafa Kemal's regime in Turkey together. There are unquestionably ways in which these resemble each other, and also ways in which they do not. It could be fatal to forget about the ways in which they differ. Generalizations about resemblances tend to be less useful than specific insights into individual behavior. If as a matter of urgent policy we have to deal with Hitler, the philosophical point that in some ways he resembles all dictators in history will be less helpful than something on the basis of which to judge how this man, here and now, is likely to react to a particular proposal or action. If we must strive to rehabilitate Vietnam, it will not help us much to be told it is part of a petrified third-generation civilization in its disintegrative stage; we will want much more concrete information. We need and want to know De Gaulle's France, not modern Western civilization. The more immediate, concrete, existential we can get, the more valuable our understanding is apt to be. Extreme generalization withdraws this kind of value from history.

If our crisis is in some ways like that of other declining civilizations, in other ways it is different, and we should know the differences as well as the similarities. Karl Jaspers pointed out important ways in which the crisis of Hellenistic civilization was not like ours: technology was then sterile, population was declining, and ancient classical civilization was much less isolated than modern Western civilization.[36] As a diagnosis of our own ills, does Toynbee's add any strength by bringing in other breakdowns? Why not tell us more about our own case, since (on Toynbee's own showing) that is what we are interested in and for which we seek a cure? More careful description of exactly how *we* got this way might be more helpful. The good physician needs the full case history of his present patient as much as he needs knowledge about disease in general. While he should possess a knowledge of the latter, it is to the former that he directs his analysis.

Toynbee's classification of civilizations encountered sharp resistance from the start. We may pass over debate about the exact number of civilizations, for Toynbee never regarded this as a finality; he was quite prepared to make adjustments in the list, and has even said that someday when our knowledge is fuller we may know hundreds of civilizations (9, pp. 204 ff.). It was the arbitrary criteria, and sometimes the very assumption that we may so divide up the seamless web of history, that affronted his critics. Less dogmatic than Spengler, Toynbee has never denied some significant contact between civilizations; yet his whole system is premised on the existence of separate units which may be compared and for which regularities in the pattern of development may be discovered. Doubts about such a procedure were widely voiced, as for example by V. Gordon Childe: "Is it legitimate or profitable to carve history into bits, label them 'civilizations' and then treat them as distinct and independent instances of general laws?" [37] Do we really have different specimens which may be compared like so many botanical specimens (Toynbee's analogy) or are they not all really leaves from the same tree (limbs from the same body, as Childe puts it)? We have, then, those to whom the entire human race is evidently a single comprehensible unit of study and any subdivisions arbitrary. We also have those who continue to insist, rather parochially, that nations are the best units of study because they do manifestly have an existence, a unity, which is not evident in civilizations. We can say what France is, and there unquestionably is a French political, a French cultural life. Who can say exactly what Western civilization is? What are its boundaries? Does it really function as a practical entity? For some purposes we may find it a useful concept, just as for other purposes (e.g., economic) we see a world system, and for still others we may have to invoke the local community; but does the civilization possess the kind of sole and unique reality status Toynbee demands we give it?

Yet it is really hard to deny that civilizations do in some sense exist and that it *is* profitable sometimes to study them. It is surely impossible to hold, with some of Toynbee's critics, that "Rome" did not exist, save as a physical location; such historians must be blind to some of the prime data of human culture. Intellectual, cultural, and literary history transcend the national boundaries of Europe, which indeed scarcely existed when modern European civilization was forged in the Middle Ages. Such fundamental configurations of thought and action as socialism, romanticism, naturalism, scientism, communism, fascism, existentialism, not to speak of Christianity, obviously must be studied in the context of all Western society, which shares basic tacit presuppositions reaching back to its classical and Judeo-Christian roots. That such a thing as Islamic civilization existed and that Chinese and Indian civilizations are independent of and different from the West are no less obvious facts.

The real weakness of Toynbee lies in his attempt to make these civilizations conform to developmental patterns. Were he content to understand them, or to show us how they differ in their outlook, we would be grateful. It has been observed that he really has little talent for this, being far less sensitive to the subtleties of cultural style than the despised Spengler.[38] In fact, the trend of his mind is oddly to run traits of civilizations together, so that Indian religion comes out looking like a slightly bent Christianity, which it surely is not. (His straightforwardly descriptive travel books, which are often very good indeed, excel in an eye for scenery, or for technical processes, more than in their insight into peoples and cultures.) Morris Watnick (in *Antioch Review*, 7 [1947], 590), who finds Toynbee's definition of civilization woefully inadequate, notes that he overlooks significant cultural divisions within civilizations, such as Nordic and Latin in the West. It might also be observed that he makes little of that change in world view from the ancient-medieval image of the cosmos (essentially the same, Aristotelian-Ptolemaic) to the modern mechanistic-Newtonian, which intellectual historians regard as basic; or to the change from an "ideational" to a "sensate" or positivist outlook (Sorokin; Comte). If Toynbee looked at Western civilization in this scarcely insignificant light, he would place ancient Hellenic and medieval civilization together, and locate the major change to a new civilization in the seventeenth-eighteenth century.

The real criteria of civilizations are subjective, not objective. Like nations, they exist in men's minds, for reasons no one can quite explain; they are words, ideas, memories, customs, affinities. Toynbee is only interested in showing that they have the same pattern of events. And this misleads him. His most serious errors, such as dividing Chinese history and Byzantine history into two civilizations, are an affront against all reason if one is thinking about the subjective bonds. Dynasties came and went, but Chinese "civilization" persisted, everyone else knows; but Toynbee must posit a new civilization when his dynasties fall in a certain way. Is there any reason to describe Jewish civilization as a "fossil" (which so offended his Jewish readers, even if Toynbee was innocent of intent to offend) if one has in mind that bond that ties people together, rather than the accidents of principalities and powers? Civilization is the Chinese family and the Jewish congregation and these things may persist even if the state crumbles. Grunebaum, protesting against Toynbee's ingenious but bizarre classifications of Islamic society, puts this well in saying that Toynbee reckons not with what civilizations are but what they did or underwent.

So there is something artificial in Toynbee's elaborate attempts to discover objectively existing slabs of time which he may hypostatize as civilizations. He wastes a great deal of effort in meaningless arguments brought on by the necessity of keeping intact his various categories. For example, in *Reconsiderations* he spends a number of pages (375–92) debating with his critics whether Roman history was, or was not, a mere appendage of Hellenic civilization.[39] Does it really matter? Most historians would agree that Greek intellectual culture continued to dominate the Mediterranean world under the Roman Empire, while Rome's special genius for warfare, government, and law gave her the political leadership. The ancient world was politically Roman and intellectually Hellenic, and was later to be spiritually Judaized. Is it worth debating whether to call it Hellenic or Roman? It is important to Toynbee only because he must make it fit the cycle of growth and disintegration.

Again, the artificiality of Toynbee's classifications strikes us when we find him (8, pp. 114–15) embarking upon an inquiry into the exact date when modern Western history began. (This is important for him because it corresponds to the beginning of breakdown.) All historians know that such periodization is arbitrary, without any other validity than convenience, and changeable according to the kind of history being written. One can place the beginning of modern history at whim anywhere from 1300 to 1800. We find ourselves saying that modern man began with Ockham, or the Fuggers, or Luther, or Descartes, or the French Revolution, depending upon what we are talking about; and we soon learn not to worry about periodization since it is so obviously a fiction. It is plain that the past is not, like geological formations, broken up into objectively existing strata or blocks. It is rather an endlessly complex continuum (as Tolstoy insisted) which we may mold in various ways depending on our purpose. But for Toynbee it must be "cut up by sharp lines into mutually exclusive parts" (Collingwood). He places the beginning of the modern era "confidently" at the end of the fifteenth century chiefly because he thinks the Italian Renaissance rejected Christianity, which is extremely doubtful; and again, later on, because at this time the "middle classes" began their sway, which is even more doubtful. But in *Reconsiderations* (p. 528, n) he decides it was in the seventeenth century that the modern world really began. There are many other cases of this sort. To most students of Russia, it is exactly the key issue and leading drama of Russian history that she could not decide which civilization she belonged to, but was torn between her multiple heritage of cultures. Toynbee decides confidently that Russia is one thing only because his schema requires it.

But that there have been rises and falls in history is as little likely to be denied as that we do seize upon such dramatic turning points in order to divide up the seamless web of history. Where Toynbee really fails is in the rigidity of his formulae. Wherever he sees what looks like a "universal state" he *must* find a civilization in its next-to-last stage of decay, and this leads to the absurdity of seeing two civilizations where there was one (China) or, alternatively, forcing the Islamic conquest to be a part of a much earlier and scarcely related civilization (which in turn made of Muhammad a member of the Syriac internal proletariat!) or requiring the Roman Empire to be Hellenic. And so throughout.

This compulsion to find perfect regularities amazes the historian who is accustomed, like Michael Oakeshott,[40] to find Clio a capricious and wayward mistress, always likely to do the unexpected. In her infinite variety she takes care never to repeat herself; it is useless to seek such repetitions as Toynbee is determined to find. If we compare the downfalls of history, we can do so honestly only by admitting that the dissimilarities are as striking as the similarities, and that they happen according to no timetable or pattern. Violence is not always suicidal, as Toynbee claims; sometimes it works. He has been frequently criticized for failing to mark the wars which in many cases accompanied the rise of civilizations: Athens, as well as Rome, was imperialistic, and the followers of Muhammad were not the last phase of an old civilization but the beginning of a new. Universal states are not always the beginning of the end; they can last for centuries and succeed by any reasonable standard of success. No rule holds in history, except the rule that for men struggling to create and to hold together structures of power and culture all things are possible. Or perhaps the rule is that at any one time, paying attention to the sum of all factors natural and human, there is a finite range of possibilities, but that this range of possibilities shifts virtually with each moment of time, so that the only possible generalizations about human societies are extremely local ones. History takes place in a super-Einsteinian field, not a sub-Newtonian one.

Toynbee's defiant reason imposes an order on the world, but that order is in him, not it. In the last analysis there seems no reason to think that the empirical world, the world of fact given to our senses, can ever be wholly or even mainly subdued to the ordering intellect. The two are, after all, quite different things. Our intellects are fired by an urge to find rules, laws, generalizations, principles of order, but this fact does not require that the real world *is* so reducible and orderable. It rather obviously is not, except partially, and imperfectly. As Henri

Marrou has observed, "La réel historique est toujours plus complexe que nos schémas unificateurs." [41] The philosopher or sociologist flees from the welter of confusing fact to formulate general principles and laws, for which he then seeks confirmatory evidence in the factual realm, only to be baffled by the inability of these generalities to cover all cases. (Of course, he may encrust himself in dogmatism and refuse to see the evidence that controverts or fails to fit his theory.) The historian, mistrusting the generalities, prefers to stay in the world of empirical reality, only to find that he can do little with it except as he borrows some hypotheses from the philosophers and sociologists. Of the need for such hypotheses, heuristic devices for handling factual reality, there can be no doubt, and Toynbee has correctly insisted upon this. As Ortega says, we imagine a reality, and then we compare this imagined reality with the facts. "If they mate happily one with another, this means that we have deciphered the hieroglyph, that we have discovered the reality which the facts covered and kept secret." [42] The charge against Toynbee the historian is that (despite his disclaimers) he has not really compared his grandiose structure of imagination with actuality, but has forced actuality to fit his structure.

Toynbee's Mind and Art

Liberal or Reactionary?

Thus the historians. Perhaps Toynbee is not writing history at all, however—the suggestion has been seriously made ("C'est magnifique, mais ce n'est pas l'histoire"). Not, at least, like other historians. Nor is he, despite his illusion, a scientist at all, but a prophet. He has written "a postcript . . . to the works of St. Augustine and Orosius, after a long delay of 1500 years," with "the vision of a seer" to which the scientific facade is irrelevant.[1] He is an artist and prophet, "playing with a sort of divine carelessness with the materials of history."[2] Since every work of history of any consequence is informed by a certain vision and reveals a certain artistry, the attempt to describe Toynbee as not historian but artist or seer seems pointless. Yet clearly his faith has impressed many as unusually intrusive. Few scholars are free from "bias," no history can be written in a vacuum, every historian begins with a bee in his bonnet (E. H. Carr)—are these truisms truer of Toynbee than of others, who may at least attempt to conceal the ideological sting that drives them to write? Or did Toynbee affront the Liberal Establishment of the academic community (at least the American academic community) by apparently adopting something other than the usual secular democratic-collectivist utopia? Yet is Toynbee really a reactionary? In some ways he is not far from a representative Anglo-American progressive.

There is no doubt about the scorn some liberals and leftists exhibited, for a Toynbee they took to be obscurantist (religious!) and irrationalist, as well as not only anti-Communist but, perhaps, antidemocratic—indeed, wholly antimodern, opposed to everything in the last four hundred years, including the great gods, Science and Technology.[3] How little Toynbee's vision of man appealed to, or was even comprehensible to a rather typical American liberal may be glimpsed in Oscar Handlin's diatribe, "In the Dark Backward"; like the Marxists, he saw only a grotesque personal outlook. One of his chief complaints was that Toynbee says no good work for democracy.[4] Another distinguished historian whose positivist cast of mind and liberal assumptions render him immune to Toynbee is H. R. Trevor-Roper, who finds only an egotistical obscurantist.[5] The Socialist Richard Crossman said of A Study of History in 1947 (by which time the first six volumes had come to his attention) that "Its grandiose terminology and its Teutonic pretensions to scientific method are merely a stucco front to a Gothic catacomb of myth and legend." [6] Myth and legend are as suspect to the mind of the liberal-progressive-socialist as are citations from the Bible and involuted prose; it likes things clear, sensible and hopeful. Neither St. Augustine nor Carl Jung appear in its gallery of favorites.

It seems somehow inevitable and unchangeable that Toynbee must annoy the Handlins and Crossmans of this world. A brief comment only on the charges of antidemocracy and irrationalism. Among Toynbee's views on democracy in A Study of History are these: it degenerates into nationalism when "imprisoned in parochial states" (4, p. 163), but the evil here is nationalism; democracy in an ecumenical form would presumably be good. He approves of democracy for destroying slavery (4, p. 140). He excoriates, as a sign of breakdown, the kind of popular education which leads to half-educated tabloid readers, and thinks an illiterate countryman who knows his Bible is more genuinely cultured than these (4, pp. 192–98). Toynbee's many pronouncements on the role of a creative minority in building and sustaining civilization leave no doubt about his belief in the necessity of leadership; but is this antidemocracy? This elite in the creative stage wins its way to leadership by its real intellectual and spiritual qualities which the people recognize and accept. When it merely rules by force and fraud, he calls it doomed. It is clear that Toynbee will tolerate no idolatry of Collective Humanity (9, p. 8); but he has respect for parliamentary representative government, and a Christian democracy seems his ideal. He regards modern democracy as indigenous to Western civilization, being rooted in Christianity ("Christian-hearted," 8, p. 214) though it has a bad form which stems from the ghost of Hellenism, is idolatrous, and issues in modern plebiscitary dictatorships (9, pp. 155, 166) as well as nationalistic wars. His 1962 lectures on *America and the World Revolution* reveal scepticism about the ability of non-European peoples to sustain parliamentary government, because it is the product of long experience and tradition; but this is no more than an empirical fact of the world today. Elsewhere he has expressed fear of the demagogue (*Hellenism*, 1959, p. 107) and doubts about the ability of the common man to know enough to pass judgment on the issues of a complex society (*America and the World Revolution*, pp. 62–64); but these are hardly more than truisms. Some of these opinions may be rather bizarre, but they are antidemocratic only if we identify democracy with secular liberalism. (Toynbee the editor and commentator on world affairs in the 1930s was of course an outstanding foe of the dictators, abhorring nazism and fascism.)

Toynbee is an unlikely "irrationalist." The whole bent of his mind, as revealed for example in his long absorption in current international affairs and his delight in an active life of travel, is quite practical and this-worldly. He is a man of much political experience, quite at home in the real world of men and events. Spengler, the poor schoolteacher, was an outsider compared to Toynbee. The demand of the ancients that historians have some practical political experience would not disqualify Toynbee nearly so much as it would most of his academic critics, who have accused him of naïveté though their own works smell of the lamp. How many of them have chatted with dictators and marched with armies?

Modern explorations of the nonrational in man affected Toynbee but little, despite the bits of Bergson and Jung he uses. As is obvious and has been frequently noted, he has not been much influenced by moderns. Despite obvious relevance to his themes Max Weber, Pareto, Durkheim, Lévi-Strauss appear as rarely in his references as the whole Freudian school, scarcely mentioned, or the existentialist-phenomenologist trend in philosophy. That Toynbee's mind is essentially Victorian is suggested by the poets he quotes. These are usually the nineteenth-century standards—Wordsworth, Browning, Meredith—or old-fashioned moderns like Robert Bridges; almost nothing from the great moderns such as Eliot or Yeats, the obvious and very quotable giants among his contemporaries, who also brooded on the decay of a culture and found their way back to ancestral truths. He is in general quite an old-fashioned rationalist in his evaluation of men and their motives, seldom resorting to Freudian or Marxian or sociological reductions.[7] Nietzschean or Sorelian glorifications of the primitive element would horrify him if he knew of them. His self-acknowledged debt to Jung consists in little more than the borrowing of some metaphors which he applies as hypotheses to historical processes—to be tested by scientific evidence. As previously remarked, it seems doubtful if he ever read much or thought deeply even about his beloved Bergson.

Is it because he has succumbed to pessimism that some liberals abhor Toynbee? But the final verdict of his historical system is optimistic. In any case, as a victim of cultural despair or a prophet of doom, Toynbee was singularly late, viewed from the level of the intellectual community. He has declared that the generation of his youth, pre-1914, had no inkling of the tragedy that struck in 1914; it was the carefree "belle époque," confident and optimistic. While there is a sense in which this is true, it is only in the most superficial sense; for, among the writers and intellectuals, this was the period of Nietzsche, Barrès, Sorel, Pareto—the disenchanted generation, whose typical school of letters was Decadence. Nor was this an attitude confined to the Continent, found only among German historians and French poets. "Upon our generation, as upon that of Rome, calamity has at last fallen," W. H. Mallock wrote in 1903 (*Is Life Worth Living?*), at which time England's best poets were dying in gutters. By the time Toynbee observed the uncomfortable plight of Western civilization, everyone else had also discovered what was then, after the First World War, too obvious to miss. The postwar era featured Joyce, Lawrence, Eliot, Proust, Aldous Huxley, Céline, and how many others whose savage indictments of their civilization make Toynbee look like a Pollyanna.

In this mood, many long before Toynbee were turning their backs on secular optimism, sometimes reverting to a neoorthodox religious position. Toynbee's indictment of Western secularism up to a point was similar to others which were among the most profound and searching conclusions of a generation that had put its hope in world wars and in apocalyptic secular ideologies, only to find them ending in slaughter and incredible barbarism without the expected millennial results. The dialectical or crisis theology of Karl Barth on the Christian side can be compared to the sceptical rationalism of Julien Benda in his *Trahison des clercs*: both found that it was gross error to put one's faith in a temporal city rather than a spiritual one, to enter into the political arena and put the precious gifts of truth at the service of worldly interests. The "clerks" had lied for and encouraged the blood feuds which pitted nation against nation or class against class. The pastor and the intellectual must serve truth beyond the interests of class or nation or party. They must keep alive spiritual values by refusing to corrupt them with mere secular ideologies. On Barth's view, the kingdom of God is utterly other than the kingdom of man, and the latter is condemned to perpetual darkness, broken only by the faint gleam of light from Christ's message, which alone crosses the unbridged gulf between God and Man.

This position seems inconsistent with any kind of secular reformism. It does not see any path of progress in human affairs; it neither approves nor condemns any economic or political order. Where Toynbee seems grossly inconsistent is in coming down finally, after all, for secular optimism, after flirting with a genuinely Barthian rejection of it.

Toynbee *is* in many ways a rather typical modern western liberal-democrat-socialist. His goals are, to the point of parody, those of what has been called the Liberal Establishment, or the average *bien pensant* liberal intellectual of modern times whose list of good causes is predictable to a degree that once led an exasperated W. L. White to speak of "knee-jerk" reactions. He wants the welfare state and the United Nations and racial equality and all the rest. One is, indeed, almost staggered by the predictability and commonplaceness of Toynbee's political opinions. Follow him down through the years, and "not a man's thought in the world keeps the roadway better than his"—a fine liberal-progressive, men-of-good-will roadway. Some may think this is not a bad roadway to keep; but anyone must be struck by the contrast between the imaginative, baroque quality of Toynbee's historical style and the flat, conformist character of his political opinions. There is not the least bit of originality in this domain, and those who would like to convict Toynbee of having a thunderously pedestrian mind can find evidence here.[8]

The naïve quality of Toynbee's political thought can be illustrated in other ways. Elie Kedourie has reproached him for a pallid idealism unwilling to come to grips with the real world: his heroes are the renouncers of power, including Tolstoy, Gandhi, and even George Lansbury. If Toynbee were consistently a renouncer of the world we could make him a saint and honor him. But what are we to think when he tells us we had better submit as quickly as possible to some global Caesar? (The typical argument is that we need a world state so badly that when we spy some savior-statesman, be he Russian or Chinese, we had better be "thankful for his arrival" and "willing to take him as we find him.")[9]

He does believe, it seems, that the historic process will have a beneficient end toward which it has all along been heading, thus placing himself by the side of Hegel and Marx as well as the Christianity of Henry Ward Beecher. And this would seem to involve him in contradictions. He has rejected and excoriated materialism, worldliness, and power, and has seemed to support a radical dualism, the logical result of which is a profound pessimism as far as concerns this world. Yet he also permits himself the belief that all will come right in the end, in a secular utopia of One World, or the City of Man. If Professor Mazlish can see Toynbee as the enemy of science and technology, Marie Swabey can find—possibly with equal justification—that he has a "touching faith in the limitless powers of technology."[10] It could be added that he has a touching faith in science, too.[11]

In piquant contrast to those who looked upon him as reactionary were the conservatives who indignantly charged Toynbee with betraying his society and offering aid and comfort to its mortal enemies. After his 1952 lectures on *The World and the West*, he was called a renegade from the camp of freedom, and received a barrage of replies including at least one book, Douglas Jerrold's *The Lie about the West* (1955). These lectures were construed as accusing the West of aggression and imperialism, with Russia appearing as the innocent and injured party. Gleb Kerensky, in a letter to *The Listener*, wondered about "the wisdom of helping to intensify the western guilt-complex and giving the camp-followers of Communism an ingenious new argument." [12] Someone else spoke of "objectivity run riot"! This was the burden of the complaint lodged by historian Jerrold against Toynbee, that he spoke no good word for the West but chose to dwell on its faults at a time when it was threatened by totalitarian dictatorship. Such scarcely contemptible achievements as civil liberty under the law, freedom of expression and constitutional government received no recognition in Toynbee's work. He did not suppose that the West could give anything to other peoples except its machines. Toynbee was certainly innocent of any intent to weaken the NATO alliance in the teeth of the "red menace," [13] but his most persistent critic among historians, Pieter Geyl, included Toynbee's bias against his own civilization in the list of charges: "I have championed against him not only the canons of the profession but . . . the vital traditions of Western civilization."

It is not too difficult to discern somewhere in the complex toils of Toynbee's mind (Janus-like, as he has described himself in *Experiences*) something of the modern intellectual's partial attraction to communism. The Futurist, he intimated in the "schism in the soul" discussion, is more promising material for Transfiguration than the Archaist or the Detached. Communism, an "anti-western religion of western origin," is the faith of the internal proletariat alienated from its no longer worthy ruling class in modern Western civilization; it is in error, but its instincts are right, its devotees really "children of light." Toynbee's whole message is passionately hostile to the Saviour with a Sword, to violence and to communism; yet he can see hope in it, too. It has in it "an element of universalism" which endears it to him. It is better than National Socialism. [14] "Can Russia Really Change?" he asked in one of his numerous popular articles (*New York Times Magazine*, July 24, 1955), and answered with an affirmative suggestion. His natural sympathies lie with the victims of Western civilization's aggressive assaults.

One Toynbee position at least has been mightily affirmed throughout in no ambivalent terms: his virtual obsession with the sin of "nation-worship," the idolatry to which modern Western man has surrendered his emptied soul. Toynbee cannot mention these "parochial" states without breaking into his vocabulary of doom and dread. In comparison with them the Universal State itself is benign. He has seemingly never remembered his original argument, in his first book of 1915, that the national communities of Europe in some respects were a step forward, a wider community, an organization of cooperation on a larger scale than anything previously known, bringing many advantages. Few would wish to quarrel with his grave concern about their continued existence today. But were they really so contemptible? They do not bear much comparison with anything known in the ancient world, which was largely built around the local community even in Roman times. That they have been quite literally the object of modern worship (flags, oaths, solemn ceremonies, and personified deifications as Britannia, Germania, the Maid, etc.) is a scandal; but was Hegel not right in seeing them as the destined vessel of modern development? At any rate, is it not fantastic to see them as "the rotting corpse of a medieval Western city-state cosmos" (3, pp. 348–501; 5, p. 642)? However that may be, Toynbee is unquestionably an internationalist, a supporter of everything ecumenical, a foe of the sovereign state—and this, one supposes, should endear him to the Left more than the Right, the liberals rather than the conservatives.

In truth Toynbee does not see much difference between the sovereign Russian state and the sovereign Western one, both worshippers of technics and power rather than spiritual things; it is a matter of indifference whether an American or a Russian Caesar presides over the coming Universal State. (He also has suggested that it might be a Chinese.) At bottom, secular ideologies whether liberal, socialist, capitalist, or whatever do not mean much to Toynbee. It is of course, only religion that counts.

Struggles With Religion

It is scarcely so strange that a young agnostic of the 1900s, as Toynbee was in his youth, should have found his way back to a religious view of the world. Surely no clearsighted contemporary could blame Toynbee for returning to the faith of his fathers. Only the peculiarly narrow-minded liberal can do that. The fate of our times, Max Weber wrote in the midst of our "Time of Troubles" (1918), is a harsh one; we are the disenchanted, we have no great art, religion has retreated from the public forum. We have the truth of science, and it is a hard truth. Let professors not try to create new religions; these will be monstrosities. If they cannot bear the fate of our times like a man, let them return to "the arms of the old churches." "In my eyes, such religious return stands higher than academic prophecy." We have surely seen through the myths of secularism, the false messiahs of earthly utopia whose way leads to slaughter and confusion, the shallow prophets of a materialistic paradise. If Toynbee joined with the likes of Karl Barth and Gilbert Chesterton and Jacques Maritain in wholeheartedly rejecting the hellish modern world for an older orthodoxy, who could blame him?

But these modern religious pessimists differ profoundly from Toynbee in that they have made no use of history, indeed have retreated from history. The old liberal theology thought that history showed a purposeful direction, and God's purposes would be realized at least partly in it; the new dialectical theology found no meaning or purpose in history. The dominant school of modern theology has therefore tended to reject or ignore Toynbee, who like the old-fashioned historical optimists sees a happy outcome. (There are, on the other hand, the recently modish theologians of secular and swinging Christianity, which turns out to be the same thing as fashionable social crusading and liquidates the Church along with its traditional doctrines. To them Toynbee can have little appeal, for he has more than once affirmed his belief in Original Sin —the wickedness and stupidity, latently at least, of human nature.) Karl Lowith, who declared that "Toynbee is neither an objective historian nor a good theologian," found incongruities in Toynbee's marriage of a scientific and objective spirit to a Christian eschatology. Like Marx, he smuggles in the eschatology in the guise of science, an inherently illegitimate procedure. We may believe in the Christian revelation; but we cannot prove it in history and science (*Meaning in History*, 1949). Similarly, John Wendon says that to convert Christianity into an ideology which will "save civilization" is to misunderstand it, for it transcends history.[15] These are the voices of today's Christian theology—post-liberal, existentialized, neo-Orthodox.[16]

But Toynbee's prophecy has two faces. On the one hand, he calls down the judgment of Jehova on an idolatrous civilization that has forgotten God in its love of pelf and power, and on a generation of intellectual vipers who spread the false gospel of a material utopia. On the other, he foresees a time when war will disappear and all men will be brothers, with leisure (supplied by industrialism) to enjoy their one True God, under a reasonably benevolent Universal (Welfare) State. Sidney Hook is among those who have seen no logical connection at all between Toynbee's religion and his politics: "Not a single one of the concrete proposals he makes for social change follows from his theological assumptions." [17] His ideas about the good society are the stock-in-trade of a modern humanitarian liberal and one can hold them without being a Christian or without accepting Toynbee's historical system.

Toynbee's religion seems to be a vague impulse toward benevolence; as one critic said, a feeling of being very religious. Toynbee holds that theology, which is only for intellectuals, is a nonessential along with rituals and the myths in which religions are encrusted. The goal of religion is to make men less self-centered, and to show them the uses to which suffering can be put. (See *An Historian's Approach to Religion*, 1956, based closely on *A Study of History*, especially vol. 7.) This is a sentimental deism of the eighteenth-century type, uninterested in theological details because convinced that all religion is at bottom the same, quite simple, and basically moralistic. This is not quite fair to Toynbee. His later "struggles" with religion obviously led him somewhat deeper, at least to a considerable knowledge of comparative religion. But frequently he is concerned to argue, dubiously, that there is really not much difference between all the world religions; for example, that Christ's role as Son of God resembles the prophets such as Muhammad or Zarathustra or the Buddha, or that the higher religions are fundamentally much alike excepting only Hinayana Buddhism—they are not competitive, but complementary. They must somehow either blend or be assembled harmoniously so as to provide the spiritual unity needed in the future global society: "A single uniform faith." [18] Nevertheless in *Change and Habit* (1966) he decided that there will, after all, be more than one religion; it would be dull otherwise, as well as illiberal (chap. 10). We can perhaps have many mansions in the house of our fourth-generation Father. All this testifies to the vagueness of Toynbee's conception of religion.

But this would appear to contradict the whole structure of Toynbee's history. He is committed to the prediction that there will be a Universal State emerging from our present time of troubles, this time on a truly global basis; and that the mingling of peoples in the ecumenical society under the shield of the ecumenical state will produce, in time, an ecumenical religion, which will be the best of all possible religions. This is how it always has been and presumably must be: the wheel of history bears religion onward and upward. While frequently denying that anyone can predict the shape of the future, Toynbee has written and talked almost constantly about the future, and puts the whole weight of his study of history behind the assurance, amounting to near certainty, that future developments must closely resemble the pattern of the past. He has, like Marx and Hegel, created an historical theology.

In *Avenues of History* (1952), Sir Lewis Namier found confusion in Toynbee's inability "to make up his mind whether to treat religion as revealed truth or a historically conditioned phenomenon." These are two different planes of truth, the latter a naturalistic one. Christianity cannot be both a revealed truth and a product of history. Historicized, it must lose its claim to transcendent truth. It can reveal itself in history, as Lessing, Herder, and Hegel thought, but can it be the *result* of an historical process, discovered by the empirical historian, as Toynbee claims? The same applies to other religions, which if they are true are true because they stem from Divine sources and have been inspired, not because the social development of a certain stage of history finds them useful. The tendency to mix holy and profane things, or confuse his role as historian and prophet, is a fundamental criticism of Toynbee. The historian describes the past and selects what is significant. In declaring religion to be "the serious business of the human race" Toynbee has made a great and a defensible claim. Who can seriously doubt that our own Age of Anxiety is searching for a faith, and that this is the most absorbing theme of our time? It is the conclusion of every serious investigator who, like Colin Wilson in *The Outsider*, conducts "an enquiry into the nature of the sickness of mankind in this mid-twentieth century." Is it not evident also that religions are today in contact and may be in process of syncretizing in some way? Were Toynbee content to describe this and call attention to its significance, he would be performing a great service. But he goes beyond this to announce the final goal of history, and thus function as prophet. Since he really does so qua humanist, he becomes most comparable to those nineteenth-century political messiahs (J. L. Talmon) who announced a religion of humanity and projected a secular utopia that would crown the historical process, bringing, in the "fulness of time," not the Last Judgment and the End of the World but the Perfect Society.[19] And of this, one would have thought, we have had quite enough.

Prophet of World Unity

Toynbee is the prophet of global unification. He is hardly alone in this field! In his book *The City of Man* (1963), W. Warren Wagar discussed a host of other such prophets, along with Toynbee. The names of F. S. C. Northrop, G. A. Borgese, Julian Huxley, Lewis Mumford, and Teilhard de Chardin spring to mind among eminent contemporaries of Toynbee. H. G. Wells, to whom Wagar devoted another volume, was dominated throughout his enormous literary output by this demon of the World State, as perhaps almost all socialists have been—whether Marxian or Fabian. (Beatrice and Sidney Webb rather consistently supported British imperialism because though perhaps wicked it was a means to the Great Society, while Communists constantly dream of their coming victory over all the world after a final apocalyptical struggle with their last foes.) Both world wars unloosed a flood of such visions of global unity.[20] Is it the Judaic-Christian tradition, with its teleological and apocalyptic tendencies, that disposes Western man to think in such terms? Is it because, having attained units as large as the nation-states, a civilization dominated by the idea of change and progress must conceive of attaining ever larger units until the ultimate end is reached? Clearly the Hindu civilization, with its characteristic indifference to time and history, feels no such impulse. Ecumenicalism is a Western pattern of thought, the natural goal of its historical and progressivist ideology, rooted in Judaism and Christianity, reappearing in modern secular philosophies such as Hegelianism and Marxism which are really derived from the same roots.[21]

Whatever its ultimate psychological origins, Toynbee like so many others was driven toward it by the two world wars and the threat of extinction in a third. "World Government" seemed the answer. It was—and is—often a facile answer, utopian and unrealistic, which assumes solutions to the real problems of world politics without facing them. Amateur war-preventers create systems by which sovereign states surrender their power to a world state, without pausing to ask how in the present state of things this can be possible. One would first have to have a cultural revolution in which men would feel a moral unity with other peoples, which they manifestly do not now feel; a socioeconomic revolution in all those portions of the globe which are centuries behind the West (if that is the proper preposition) in development; and a political miracle which would somehow square the circle of achieving national security without surrendering national power. A world government, as Toynbee understood, has to be a product of history, it cannot be conjured into existence by phrases.

Though not guilty of the worst form of utopian one-worldism, Toynbee has typically thought about international affairs in a quite idealistic, perhaps semiutopian way, indeed, an often incredibly naïve way. He has tended to moralize: where others see the tragic conflict of "right with right" as Hegel said, Toynbee sees right and wrong positions. The Arabs are right, the Jews are wrong; the Vietcong are right, the Americans are wrong. In his *Experiences*, we read such judgments as: "Israeli colonialism . . . is one of the two blackest cases in the whole history of colonialism in the modern age," and that the Americans are trying "to build an American colonial empire in Eastern Asia." Toynbee the moralist thinks that war is wicked (ibid., pp. 82–83); and Toynbee the historian adds, more dubiously, that war is caused by wicked "aggressors" (*Study*, 9, 234–87). In the *Study*, aggressive war is never mentioned in connection with growth and creativity, but only in connection with breakdown and disintegration—which will hardly stand scrutiny, as critics have noted. Toynbee's aversion to violence is commendable, but it is a falsification of history to assert that all growths are peaceful (or nonaggressive) and all declines militaristic. Fond of poetic metaphors, Toynbee might have cited Shakespeare: some rise by sin, and some by virtue fall. But in *A Study of History* civilizations always rise by virtue and fall by sin (war). In the growth phase there was legitimate self-defense, only later, wicked "militarism."

Disenchanted with the League of Nations (which he thought had "failed to avert the Second World War" and which he came to think of as essentially a balance-of-power device) [22] Toynbee announced after World War II that "Mankind will either achieve political unification or will perish"; the choice lies between the world state and "mass suicide." It was not, in the age of the atom bomb, a startling or unusual opinion, especially right after 1945, before the Cold War chilled the atmosphere. (It seems almost incredible today that in 1945 the United States offered to turn all its atomic knowledge and equipment over to an international authority.) World government has become increasingly chimerical in an age dominated by the rival power blocs of Russia and the United States and by the extremely nationalist *jeunes états* of newly independent peoples. But Toynbee has continued to repeat it in many a public utterance, down to his recent books (1966, 1969). He tied it, of course, to his whole historical theology. Such unity is man's destiny as revealed by the record of past civilizations.

He has not been entirely consistent in the details of the coming world religion, society, and government. In *Civilization on Trial* (1948) Toynbee held that "religion is likely to be the plane" on which world unity will first manifest itself (p. 94). In *Change and Habit* (1966), however, he said that political unity will come first, forced by practical conditions, while there is still a variety of religions. The *Study of History* system evidently has universal states preceding universal religions; it is the decay of the creative minority, leading to force and militarism, which causes the masses to withdraw their appreciative mimesis and secede from the body politic to experiment in violent futurisms before at length finding their way to religion. If the last of Toynbee's universal states is like the others, it will be the militaristic achievement of a dominant minority which has lost its creativity. Followed by a universal church, it might wither away (Toynbee's version of Marx's utopia), leaving pure church. This universal religion is a result of the minglings of peoples in the cultural cosmopolitanism of the universal society.

The universal state occupies an ambiguous place in Toynbee's thought, as his reconsideration of it in volume 7 suggests. A product of breakdown, it normally leads to disintegration, is the product of militarism and a decline of creativity; but it ends the scandal of "parochial" states as well as creating the necessary conditions for higher religions and universal churches. The "oecumenical empire" is "Man's worship of collective human power in its least maleficent and least unedifying form," shining by comparison with the "parochial states" of the "time of troubles." On the other hand, often Toynbee sees this ecumenical welfare state in a "doleful light," an "idol . . . erected in a still discarded Christianity's place," probably ruled by an American or Russian Caesar (*An Historian's Approach to Religion,* pp. 93, 219). Historians of antiquity have accused him of excessively hero-worshipping Alexander the Great, and he does appear to admire the world-conquering hero whenever somewhat "enlightened." He has on other occasions speculated that not Russia or America but China will form the nucleus of the future world state (*Change and Habit,* p. 158); and that it will not be a unitary state but a voluntary association, loosely binding together what Spaak called "the great human communities." If the Universal State came about by force it would be cursed and doomed; it must be voluntary (*Between Niger and Nile,* p. v). This last in particular involves him in a large inconsistency, and elsewhere he has declared that we must be prepared to create the world-state before it is democratically possible: democracy is a slow and difficult achievement, and the urgent need to escape "mass suicide" cannot wait on this, we will have to have a dictator, an Augustus or a Liu P'ang.[23] But Toynbee knows that "we cannot foretell the future" (*World and the West,* p. 99) and it would be absurd to expect him to see the exact shape of things to come. Yet he has continued to predict that in the long run the world must unify or die, and that it is in fact proceeding toward unification in some form.

Is this a reasonable prophecy? If Toynbee is claiming there are two options, and no more than two—we must unify the world or all die—he is plainly not telling the truth. It is possible that even if they put together some sort of world federation, men would still fight each other, for the roots of conflict lie deep and no more mechanical adjustment can destroy them. It is possible that even if war continues and destroys part of the human race, new civilizations will arise. It is even possible that men might learn to live together in peace while retaining their national units. No man, not even Toynbee, can predict the future; and his two possibilities plainly do not exhaust the list of conceivable alternatives.

What seems obvious to the historian who is looking

squarely at mankind as it is today is that the World City is as yet far, far away, if it ever can exist. Men have still not solved the problem of living together in communities as large as the nation-state. While secession plagues Africa, the result of loyalties to tribal units more parochial than the nation-state, Asiatic nations like India and Pakistan are riven by communal and religious schisms; their problem is to "make Indians" or Pakistani, and this looks like it will take a long time. Black nationalism in the United States is the greatest threat to the stability of the world's most powerful nation. Ibo rebels in Nigeria, Chinese in Malaysia, Muslims in India, Arab guerrillas harassing Israel, Vietnamese fighting Americans, all the many troubled areas of the world do not show us people clamoring to overthrow nationalism in order to join the World State, but people seeking parochial self-determination or struggling *for* nationalism. The Communist bloc is struggling desperately and evidently unsuccessfully against centrifugal tendencies, despite its ideological cement and its terroristic methods. The world has far less unity than it did three-quarters of a century ago when Western imperialism provided a sort of *pax Britannica* for the world, when African and Asian nationalism was only beginning to stir, and when Europe itself was not riven by bitter ideological divisions between states. If the historian must venture prophecy, looking hard at present trends he would have to say, surely, that the movement is in the opposite direction: not more unity but more diversity in the world.[24] Nationalism was never stronger, as Abba Eban pointed out to Toynbee.

As a practical matter it is impossible to conceive any of the great powers—or many of the lesser ones—signing over control of their destinies to a superstate. The United Nations has been rendered impotent by the unwillingness of the powers to grant it armed strength even for specific and temporary purposes. Writing about world government, another distinguished British historian, Sir Llewellyn Woodward, noted in 1955 that a real world-state would mean giving up the West's higher standard of life, and also would create a potential super-tyrant, "remote, gigantic, and impersonal, spreading its plans like a quilt over us" (*Listener*, September 29, 1955). The frightening amount of power now in existence cannot be abolished; if it is transferred to a single world-state that power becomes capable of subjecting everyone to the most monstrous tyranny yet known in the world. A combination of self-interest and fear must make the existing political components as little likely to surrender themselves to such a superstate as anything we can well conceive. Even nuclear war is, unhappily, much more probable.

It is equally hard to detect any grounds well in the direction of Toynbee's world religion. The Christian church has perhaps become more ecumenical; but it is hard to see it blending with Islam or Buddhism,[25] or to see any of these conquering Africa, much less China or Russia. One can imagine the African world producing religions which blend traditional African rites with Christianity, Islam, and secular ideologies from the West.[26] One can imagine the Communist world slowly losing its Marxian ideological fanaticism to become almost as pluralistic and pragmatic as the West. One can imagine the West, after all religions and ideologies, after even existentialism, existing without any faith, as Technocratic Man. One can imagine many things. Can one accept Toynbee's vision of One World and One Faith as anything other than a vision without relationship to reality? In part it is an unwarranted projection onto the future, of something like what happened in the past (Hellenic-Roman model); in part it is simple political messianism.

A recent survey of world religions by an expert in the field concluded that "religious life is likely to get more, rather than less, variegated in the immediate future" and that "It is hardly likely that a real unity will be achieved in the foreseeable future."[27] To which Toynbee might well reply that "there is all the time in the world," and eventually unity must come whatever the winds of the moment. One cannot predict short-term currents. (Toynbee himself was an extraordinarily bad prophet when, in 1965, he declared Nigeria to be "a happy augury for the future of the human race" because of its successful merger of peoples "into something like a single family" [*Between Niger and Nile*, pp. 17–22]. The massacre of the Ibos the next year, followed by secession and civil war, showed how disrespectful Clio could be of the global prophet.) But one can be sure of major long-term drifts. We may be unable to predict the weather from day to day but we are certain of the secular cycle. It is clear that the religions of the world are mingling more, that there are now American Buddhists and Asiatic cardinals of the Roman church, and that this may be expected to continue. That it will take time is only to be expected.

> Technology can bring strangers physically face to face with one another in an instant, but it may take generations for their minds, and centuries for their hearts, to grow together.[28]

If at present the disintegration of Christianity (as an organized Church, in an age of "secular Christianity," or even "atheist Christianity," of chaos in the Church of Rome and extreme subjectivity everywhere) seems possible, this could well be the preliminary to a reassembly of elements of Christianity with other world religions and religious philosophies such as existentialism. Who is to say that Toynbee is wrong in his intuition that world unity will first manifest itself on the religious plane? It is at least certain that even now very strange things are spiritually in process: veritably a world revolution.

In this great process of building what Father Teilhard de Chardin called the "noösphere," Toynbee may well be too narrow in his outlook, for he seems to include only the "higher religions," which he has from time to time numbered as low as four and as high as twelve. But the great French comparative religionist Mircea Eliade has spoken of our "dialogue with the primitive" and has included these so-called lower religions in his synthesis of world religion.[29] Toynbee has a curious habit of excluding ideas as "dead" if they belonged to a civilization (i.e., political society) that perished. He regards Platonism and Stoicism as dead, for example (*An Historian's Approach*, p. 139), and does not include primitive religions in his purview at all. As in the Hegelian dialectic, what has been superseded by a higher synthesis no longer exists except as it is contained in that synthesis. But the real world is more complex than that. No idea that ever existed and was recorded can die; it survives, or it may awaken, it may rise from the dead after centuries of slumber. For example, Platonism revived in the Renaissance to play a decisive role in the Scientific Revolution as well as, perhaps, in the Reformation. John Maynard Keynes went back to discarded theories of Thomas Malthus in in his creative new economics of the 1930s. Father Teilhard (who greatly admired Toynbee) had a vision of all these ideas—no voice wholly lost—blending together at the Last Day. Toynbee, as prophet, may be criticized for restricting the field of the noösphere much too narrowly. And, on the other hand, he can certainly be taken to task for understating the differences in religions: the gulf between the Judaic-Christian-Islamic monothesistic, prophetic, and messianic type and the Indic-Buddhist which is in so many ways directly the opposite, seeing no transcendent deity, no personal salvation, no meaning in history. Is it really possible for authentic Christianity to accept syncretization with very different religions on the basis of what one critic indignantly calls "a naïve, undifferentiated idea of religion whose only common denominator is 'a feeling of utter dependence' "?[30] A chorus of Western theologians answers "No."

Can we really be spiritually nourished by a Universal Civilization? Would we be happy in the World Welfare

State? Is not religion itself something that needs to be rooted in a specific tradition, as local as possible? Today, when the great modern myth of nationalism in some places is undeniably showing signs of weakening, regionalism and local autonomy are more vital than they have been for a long time—more vital than "pan-" movements. The instinct to find roots in face-to-face relationships and create true communities, which have to be small, has reasserted itself in a contemporary humanity weary of bigness and the dehumanization that inevitably goes with it. Thus a rejoinder to Toynbee. One of the most civilized minds to address himself to the criticism of Toynbee, Sir Ernest Barker, protested against his rather totalitarian unity-urge: "My desire is for the many-coloured energetic play of a plurality of open national states." There is really no answer to questions about the shape of the future. Yet one's bottom feeling is that man, torn by conflicting impulses as he always is, will never find an everlasting resting place. He aspires to universality but also to locality, and when he has one he wants the other. Given a Universal Welfare State without war and with a unified religion compounded somehow of all the best ideals of human history, the perverse creature would in all likelihood find it intolerable and rebel against it, demanding diversity and local independence. Certainly he has in the past found peace intolerable and cried for war: to a large extent, indeed, this happened in 1914.

If a man is tired of London, said Dr. Johnson, he is tired of life, because in London is everything that life has to offer. No doubt Johnson was provincial. But if a man is tired of his own civilization, can he find joy in the ecumene? Toynbee has stated flatly that he "does not like" Western civilization. (An attitude typical of the modern intellectual. "Europe bores me"—André Gide, 1894.) Is it possible that he simply does not like Man? Is anything bigger likely to be better? Toynbee's own analysis of growth, we recall, found that expansion accompanies spiritual decay, universalism means the cheapening of culture. If it is a truism to say that we all now live in the Global Village, it is another, and perhaps a truer one, to say that we must confront our destiny in our own neighborhood. And if the World State could not bring spiritual contentment, could it preserve peace? And, since Toynbee assures us that man is free, is this possibly unpleasant and ineffective juggernaut really necessary? We may be sure that Toynbee would have answers to all these queries, because from first to last he has fervently supported universalism.

The Art of History

The question of style is an important one in Toynbee's case because of the obvious and extensive stylization. That is to say, A *Study of History* is not a straightforward statement of propositions, by a long shot. If it were, it would be a fraction of the length, and it would be cast in very different language. For all he may say in justification of his metaphors, they are not just useful tools of scientific truth, they are imaginative constructions. If a reader is impervious to the charm of Toynbee's style he may well think the *Study of History* a preposterously inflated and exceedingly pretentious piece of work, which could just as well have been stated in one-tenth of the space and without resort to the mystifying vocabulary. Why talk about "the idolization of an ephemeral past" when what is meant is simply getting in a rut, or use terms like *Hybris* and Atē for plain overconfidence? And what is the use of multiplying garish examples of such obvious human weaknesses? Sententious, attacking straw men and presenting trite notions in solemn verbiage; wordy, elaborating the obvious—such are the complaints filed against Toynbee. Sorokin remarked that the work "could have been compressed without losing anything in the clearness and completeness of its theory," as indeed Somervell's abridgement proved, while anti-Toynbeeans such as Walter Kaufmann never fail to sneer at his "gentle art of saying nothing, with flamboyant rhetoric," or (E. F. J. Zahn) his "edifying truths and truisms," his pseudoprofundity.[31] And one can see all too easily what they mean. Toynbee does often seem to cover an embarrassing triviality of thought with an extravagance of metaphor.

This wordiness in elaborating the obvious grew rather worse in the later volumes of A *Study of History.* In one typical passage covering several pages, Toynbee draws examples from the ancient Greeks, the French in North Africa, African Negroes, Vietnamese, the Dutch in Indonesia, and the whites in South Africa to illustrate the point that "the representatives of an aggressively radioactive civilization that has been successful in penetrating an alien body social are prone to succumb to the *hybris* of the Pharisee who thanks God that he is not as other men." He means that colonial rulers are apt to be snobbish, and we hardly need to be convinced. If the early volumes are at least charged with the excitement of an eager quest for answers to important questions, the later ones reveal the flattening out of a mind that has found its answer, and repeats it by rote —an answer that turns out to be rather conventional.

Despite all this, Toynbee must be judged highly as a literary artist. The first volumes represent a work of art the reading of which has been for countless numbers a memorable, an enriching experience even if they were unconvinced by the formal argument. The texture is astonishingly rich. Toynbee digresses, elaborates, and illuminates the whole with a vast and charming erudition. It is something like *The Anatomy of Melancholy* mixed with Bayle's *Dictionary* and suffused with a Saint-Simonian anecdotal quality. Though Toynbee has spoken of his style as if it came from the Greeks and Romans, it seems securely anchored in the great English tradition, but it draws on the literature of the world. Like Joyce, he "took all knowledge for his playground," and he just about got away with it. R. H. Tawney spoke of the "fertility, vitality, energy, inexhaustible élan" of the first volumes; this was widely felt at the time.[32] Disenchantment came with familiarity and repetition (undoubtedly Toynbee has written far too much, and cheapened his product), but the magic still exerts its effect on young minds who come fresh to A *Study of History*. The intensely personal, easily parodied Toynbee style, with its standard devices (the ornate alias, the repetitious incantation, the Biblical footnote) can badly put off those not mesmerized by it. But, if we ask for evidence of its success, to its very large number of readers we must add the wide influence of its phrases. Toynbee's historical metaphors have invaded our vocabulary and thus affect our thinking: Challenge-and-Response, Time of Troubles, Rout and Rally, Schism in the Soul, and many others. There is no question about the effectiveness of his figures drawn from myth and literature and applied to historical processes, though there are obvious dangers in such a practice. (Who can gainsay Lord Palmerston's dictum that "Half the wrong conclusions at which mankind arrive are reached by the abuse of metaphors"?) The imagination which has supplied them in such profusion must be rated highly in its province. These phrases glow in our minds, faintly smoldering with a doomsday quality; we do not feel like objecting much when it is asserted that Toynbee's work must be compared not to that of scholarly historians but to the poetic epics of man's fate: Dante's *Divine Comedy* and Milton's *Paradise Lost*.[33]

Toynbee's taste can lapse appallingly at times. At a rather solemn moment in volume 7 (p. 496), when he has confronted us with the awful prospect of self-destruction today at the hands of "a weapon of unprecedented potency [which] had fallen into an unregenerate Humanity's hands," and has asked "Where, in these appalling circumstances, was Man to look for access to the life that is the gift of God (Rom. vi, 23)?" he finds "a gleam of light" in some lines not from any great poet, but from one Martyn Skinner, who is one of the few poets later than George Meredith whom Toynbee often quotes, but whose verse is surely by contemporary standards almost as appalling as the circumstances from which he is summoned to rescue us; a true candidate for admission to *The Stuffed Owl*. Toynbee's literary taste, this side of Robert Browning, is deplorable; poetically, he is an archaist worshipping the ghost of an ephemeral past.

But it would be ungracious not to recall also the many times Toynbee *does* supply just the right quotation, more than likely from Homer or Sophocles or St. Paul; or the apt metaphoric analogy, probably from a myth or from a process in nature. This is the genius that seldom failed him in the first six volumes of the *Study*. The keenness of Toynbee's natural eye may be seen in the travel books: try, for example, the description of the Indus River bursting out of its gorge at Kalabagh to stretch itself on the plain (*Between Oxus and Jumna*, pp. 162–63). Zest for life and joy in natural beauty combines here with a nice economy of phrase that is not commonly thought of as a Toynbee trait. But his prose, at least in the earlier volumes of *A Study of History*, is not loose; it is his subject that is voluminous, not Toynbee. In his own image, he tried to drink the ocean dry; he set himself an impossible task. He failed. But there have been successes that were far less glorious.

Historian for Our Time?

Conservative, grave, and meditative, Toynbee was a favorite of the fifties. The raucous sub-romanticism of the sixties, with its cult of youth and activism, its only slightly veiled anti-intellectualism, its contempt for tradition, has temporarily passed him by. Neither Hippies nor New Leftists could be expected to have any patience with this immense learning, this immersion in the heritage, all leading to the advice that we go back to the fountains of religion. Very "square," indeed. Toynbee is an archetypal Old Wise Man, not a young angry one. But we cannot seriously consider such fads of the moment in evaluating a major reputation. What will the responsible future have to say about Toynbee?

His once formidable and still considerable repute rested upon a remarkable combination of qualities. He offered an explanation for our present time of troubles, together with a prescription for surmounting it. He presented a total view of history. ("The doctrine which will sufficiently explain the whole of the past will inevitably obtain, in consequence of this achievement alone, the mental governance of the future," August Comte once wrote.) He broke through what Whitehead called the "intimate timidity of professional scholarship" to present truly exciting visions of man and society on a large scale. He combined seemingly incredible erudition with literary artistry and bold imagination. He was welcomed by a public aroused to keen interest in the past by the gravity of the modern crisis. (People turn to history at moments of such crisis, Allan Nevins wrote in *The Gateway to History*, "when great events waken them to their most serious and responsible temper.") He was equally in tune with his times in expanding the cultural frontiers of Western man to encompass the rest of the world. And he showed what one mind could do, in an age of computerized knowledge and institutionalized research. Let us sum up the merit of these claims.

That our civilization is indeed in the throes of disintegration no thinking person can reject as a serious possibility. The manifestations are too obvious for anyone to miss. The overt signs of it in riots, demonstrations, drugs, pornography, alienation, "dropping out" are only slightly more noticeable than such things as the death of art and literature, or at least its radical division into a weird minority protest and a mindless majority entertainment; the fragmentation of knowledge involving the destruction of any integrated vision of the world; the triumph of scepticism over all belief leading to desperate existentialist experiments in belief in belief itself, which do not work either. Those who worry about extinction in nuclear war are not more numerous than those who see man "destroyed by the instruments he has fashioned to minister to his own needs" (Karl Jaspers), enslaved by the machine, made into a machine; or poisoned by the fumes of his industrial processes, deprived of space and water and air, slain by the imbalances of nature his technological juggernaut creates. And so on.

This process has been evoked or recorded in countless novels, poems, and tracts; it is perpetuated in our serious literature (today largely one of black pessimism) and memorialized in our philosophy (based, at least in its existential form, on the meaninglessness of the world and the absurdity of being). But it has never yet received its proper history. Toynbee is not really a very good historian of this process. It is surprising that both he and Spengler felt impelled, not to describe and carefully analyze this Western decadence, but to theorize about the decay of all civilizations. Perhaps in so doing they were trying to exorcize this demon of decline. Polybius long ago spoke of the soteriological function of history: "The memory of other people's calamities is the clearest and indeed the only source from which we can learn to bear the vicissitudes of Fortune with courage." It is, in brief, reassuring to learn that many others have fallen too. It may help to diminish what Mircea Eliade has called "the terror of history" if we believe, with Toynbee, not only that others have fallen but that there is a forward movement as dying societies pass on the torch of their spiritual achievement, wrung from their suffering.

In writing his great history Toynbee was, then, reacting to the predicament of our times and doing something to deal with it, but he was not functioning as its historian, and we still await an account of equal brilliance and scope which will describe the decline of the West and not attempt to subsume it under vague general laws. Such a history would not find it necessary to bring in other civilizations except as analogies used to illuminate its subject, the Decline of the West. It would show us exactly how these fatal declines in creativity and schisms in the soul and parochial divisions leading to suicidal militarism arose, which Toynbee in fact scarcely does at all. But no such history will be able to ignore Toynbee's great opus.

Indeed, no student of society and culture can ignore Toynbee. In the fine phrase of James Feibleman, "He has made it impossible to see the world, and especially human history, henceforth, without looking to some extent through his eyes." [34] His least questionable achievement is to have provided a store of metaphor to use in the understanding of human affairs, which strikes the imagination and sticks to the mind; and, further, in stimulating curiosity and additional investigation along these lines. As a revealer of scientific "laws" he quite failed; and his orderly and purposive pattern of the past must be seen as largely the creation of his imagination. It may be true that his extensive lay-following stems chiefly from this assertion of a "transcendent and universal meaning in history." [35] But it is impossible for the sceptical modern mind to believe in this meaning, revealed for us by Toynbee the Prophet, who plays God; [36] if history has an ultimate meaning, there is no way we can detect it, and no such system as Toynbee's can withstand criticism. At the same time we must recognize the force of his indictment of the modern specialist, and the need for wholeness. In a time of troubles such as we are experiencing today there is a need for broad historical works, even prophetical ones, which professional historiography does not meet and which will be created by someone. Better Toynbee than others one might name!

A political theorist has recently argued that philosophies of history are not objectively demonstrable, but are necessary to provide a "framework of meaning" to all social science.[37] In other words, the larger structures of thought within which our inquiries function, at least in human affairs, are imaginative creations, though we may forget this. In brief, we live by myths. Toynbee appears to be in tune with linguistic philosophy of the most advanced sort in arguing that our terminology is all metaphor, all myth; the abstract words we use, and which we may think are "rational concepts," are just old figures of speech whose origin we have forgotten. So those who complain that Toynbee's purported science is really myth may miss the point. So is any such structure. The only question is whether the myth is usable, effective, fruitful. And the answer to this question is that much if not all of Toynbee is.

The specialists shrink from the big questions. The Byzantinists do not presume to tell us why Byzantium fell; they are too busy explaining why Leontius rebelled against Justinian II, and a thousand other matters. If it be said that someday when all these lesser questions are answered the big ones can be, the answer is that the lesser questions are never exhausted and in fact breed ever lesser ones ad infinitum. Besides, what are we to do until "someday"? Toynbee is right in saying that men do yearn for orientation from history and that this need is not met by most professional historiography with its cult of archives and its infragroup professional standards. (Nor, of course, by amateurs anxious to exploit the melodramatic and lecherous for profit.) His striving for wholeness is commendable, and who can deny that he is in the right when he pleads that "Somehow we have to break down the artificial compartments between the 'disciplines' and to rediscover how to study human affairs as the unity that they are in fact"?[38] This has been his lifelong mission and, unrepentant, he says in *Experiences* that he is glad he has not been a specialist. He can elicit much sympathy these days even from the professionals.[39] Is his call for a "deliberate cultivation of intellectual versatility"[40] not worth trying as a cure for the deadening hyper-specialization of our age?

With the grave humor he can sometimes summon, he once passed his verdict on that dusty answer to the imposing demands made on the modern scholar, collective or institutionalized research:

> God breathed the breath of life into Adam, but it might be beyond the compass of even divine omnipotence to make a living soul out of a committee.[41]

This characteristic remark reminds us of what a personal achievement his work has been. With all its magnitude, it has always been one man's Promethean challenge to human limitations, a defiant attempt to gulp down the ocean; it could not possibly have been written by a committee. A committee might have avoided the factual errors which unhappily clog A *Study of History*; it could never have informed it with the uncanny charm that makes the book a work of art and, undoubtedly, a "possession for all time."

We need not repeat that Toynbee was right and deserves credit for reminding us how inadequate national history is, how necessary it is for most purposes to take civilizations as the unit of study rather than political states or nations; and for insisting that we recognize the existence and importance of civilizations other than our own. He can claim no great originality on either score; for Voltaire first urged the latter proposition more than two centuries ago, and when Matthew Arnold wrote in 1865 that Europe is "for intellectual and spiritual purposes, one great confederation, bound to a joint action and working to a common result," he asserted what no civilized person ever doubted prior to the bizarre upthrust of a vulgar nationalism which since about 1880 has accompanied the rise of modern barbarism. A genuine historian, said Taine, is not sure that his own civilization is perfect, and lives as gladly out of his country as in it. As for urging an expansion of historical outlook to embrace other civilizations of the world, one of Toynbee's mentors, Lord Bryce, declared in 1913, at the International Congress of Historical Studies, that "Whatever happens in one part of the globe now has a significance for every other part. World History is tending to become one history." This was a truism even before the two world wars drove the lesson home. But not many have ever done more than Toynbee to "enlarge the scene of world history" and embrace other peoples in its scheme (N. Bammate). Those who, like Lawrence Stone and Walter Kaufmann, otherwise criticize him severely have applauded him for helping to break the bonds of our parochialism. Though too much purely national history marred by a narrow outlook is still written (American historians especially might take note), these revolutions have been safely accomplished; we are unlikely ever again to be unaware of the non-Western world or Euro-centered in our view of it. This revolution is a part of the development of our times and countless others have contributed to what is almost a natural process, yet Toynbee's special place of honor in the history of this widening outlook seems secure.

For all the grandeur of his achievement, there is a very real danger that Toynbee will appear to posterity as no more than a curiosity, and will exert little influence; he may come nearer to joining Buckle and Spencer than Marx and Weber. Erich Heller once remarked of Spengler that he had achieved a "highly topical oblivion," and this would seem also to be Toynbee's fate: everybody remembers that he should be forgotten. Though, as we have remarked, certain of his phrases stick in our vocabulary, there is a tendency for him to be overlooked by the specialists. He does not often appear in the references or bibliographies of standard works on the various periods and areas of history, nor in textbooks on world religions, and so forth. Insofar as there is such a thing as "World History," Toynbee has to be a founding father of it; but is there? The subject as taught in American high schools or presented in less imaginative textbooks is usually no more than the consecutive narrations of different histories, with suggestions of some reciprocal influence— nothing like the Toynbeean system of common laws of development and a grand spiritual goal.[42] If Toynbee's own version of World History manifestly will not pass critical scrutiny, the inferior product which threatens to take over this dubious market is an unworthy legacy of his influence. As for Toynbee the prophet of world unity or a world religion, his ideas here are too commonplace to stand out from a host of other similar ones.

In brief, by trying to be jack-of-all-trades he became master of none, and for better or worse we live in an age of scholarly and intellectual tradesmanship. Will the general public, the "educated laity," remember him? Its memory today is notoriously short. It is strongly disposed to trendiness. No longer in vogue, Toynbee has been largely forgotten by this public, though he still tends to bob up on prophetic occasions with appropriate platitudes (as witness the recent moon landing, when his remarks were widely circulated in the American press). This role as a kind of public-affairs laureate will not provide a firm basis for immortality.

Doubtless Toynbee's natural place is as one of these "men of letters" who, according to a recent book, rose in the nineteenth century and have since fallen.[43] Among historians he resembles Macaulay, Carlyle, or Morley more than he does the Oscar Handlins and Lawrence Stones of today, whose scorn for him knows no bounds. He has appealed to such anachronistic all-around sages of the modern era—amateur historians and secular prophets—as Lewis Mumford. It is a fast disappearing type. It drew its readership and intellectual sustenance from the nineteenth-century *haute bourgeoisie*, a class both moneyed and serious; an age when general reviews (from the *Edinburgh* and *Westminster* to *Spectator* and *Nation*, in Britain) published serious intellectual fare for a respectable reading public. Historians who were basically "men of letters," not professional research scholars, combined readability with a flair for stimulating ideas and were often short on factual reliability or depth of research, though some of them managed to be sufficiently energetic on this score. They filled a necessary place in the literary culture of which, being essentially civilized minds, they were a part. We miss them today. We miss the civilized cultures to which they belonged—the "House of Intellect," the "Traditions of Civility." Toynbee's popularity was an indication that a literate public of broad and serious interests may still exist, if writers with broad and serious interests will but seek it.

The one nagging doubt about Toynbee that stays to the end is not his factual inaccuracy—a remediable failing—or his prophetic imagination, or anything else except the suspicion of bad faith associated with his tendency to twist the past to fit his prejudices. This is not a matter of a personal vision or a point of view, which every historian must have. It is rather an at times willful blindness to the evident state of things, caused by his determination to force istory to prove his points. History is of course all too susceptible to distortion. It can mean many things, but it cannot mean anything, otherwise we are at the mercy of politicans and cranks, and history becomes not a guide and fulcrum but a tool of fanaticism and prejudice. There is a line of truth at the heart of history which we must not bend unless we are to break our whole claim on rationality. The Toynbee prejudices are well known, and they are doubtless commendable: abhorrence of war, dislike of power, yearning for a perfect kingdom of brotherly love, and so forth. But war and power and hate are in fact human and bound up with every human situation. History is untidy and distressing and hateful, far more than Toynbee will admit.

There are other ways in which his prejudices distort history. The significant point about this is that for most other historians, investigation is a corrective of prejudice. That is its great value. Life being as it is, it is almost impossible for an honest investigator to emerge from a thorough study of a man or episode or age with any simple like or dislike intact. Your vision of the French Revolution or the New Deal or Cromwell or Lenin cannot be entirely one-sided if you have really studied these men and events. Reality usually defeats any naïve glorification or vilification such as ideological or religious passion implants in our minds. But Toynbee does not normally examine the record in this way; it is his characteristic method, as we know, not to see one episode in its specificity and context, but to pull events from their context in order to compare them with other events and thus arrive at generalizing laws. It is a method calculated to confirm one in one's prejudices. Toynbee's method does not allow history to function as a corrective of such prejudice for one is always proceeding as if one's prejudices are true.

Thus we are back to the central objection, the feeling of "this will never do" which worried even the very first reviewers almost swept away by the sheer virtuosity of Toynbee's performance. Clearly Toynbee did fail, in his primary goal, whatever incidental successes be achieved and however glorious the failure. One doubts that anyone else will ever take up this particular quest. A *Study of History* would seem to share with *Finnegans Wake* the quality of being so fantastic a tour de force that no one can continue in its direction. It will stand there for posterity to gaze at, in amazement or amusement. Its phrases and insights will join the vocabulary of literate men. Historians of thought and culture will see it less as the last desperate endeavor of modern positivism to reduce human affairs to an exact science than as a statement of contemporary anguish in the teeth of cultural decay. As such, it spoke on the right side: for the spirit against the machine, for the brotherhood of man against selfish nationalism, for wholeness against fragmentation. But, as the last, it was an unwarranted shortcut, the product of a romantic ego determined to swallow the sea of knowledge all by itself—surely, when we come down to it, an *atē* or intoxication, a most un-humble and un-Christian spirit, a defiance of all of Toynbee's proclaimed moral principles. Historians reading *A Study of History* will continue to feel, as did Sir Ernest Barker, that

> I was not walking the familiar chambers of a House of Time that I knew; I was treading the "vasty halls" of a system of categories which, to me, were the fabric of a vision."

A generation after Toynbee, one marked by a great deal of activity in the "analytical" philosophy of history, knowledgeable historians and philosophers are prepared to agree on at least one thing, that we cannot make *total* sense of the past. We can make *some* sense of it, but only by abandoning the holistic vision as an impossible romantic dream. Like Karl Marx's, Toynbee's system of history was one of the last febrile products of the romantic imagination, masquerading as science.

Notes

Introduction

1. J. H. Meisel, in *Journal of Modern History*, 32 (September 1960), 266.
2. R. H. Tawney, in *International Affairs*, 18 (November 1939), 801.
3. *New Statesman and Nation*, 18, September 23, 1939, 433.
4. E.g., M. F. Ashley Montagu, ed., *Toynbee and History* (Boston: Porter Sargent, 1956), Edward T. Gargan, ed., *The Intent of Toynbee's History* (Chicago: Loyola University Press, 1961).
5. A. J. Toynbee, *Reconsiderations: A Study of History*, 12 (London, New York, Toronto: Oxford University Press, 1961).
6. Ibid., pp. 136–43.
7. See, e.g., O. F. Anderle, "A Plea for Theoretical History," *History and Theory*, 4, no. 1 (1965), 48.
8. Edward T. Fox, "History and Mr. Toynbee," *Virginia Quarterly Review*, 36 (1960), 456.

1 — Career and Writings

1. There was another uncle by marriage who was a well-known chemist—see *Experiences* (London and New York: Oxford University Press, 1969), pp. 293–305.
2. On the older Arnold Toynbee, see F. C. Montague, *Arnold Toynbee*, Johns Hopkins University Studies in History and Political Science, 7, no. 1 (Baltimore: Johns Hop-

kins Press, 1889); the memoir by Benjamin Jowett printed in Arnold Toynbee, *The Industrial Revolution of the Eighteenth Century in England, Popular Addresses, and Other Fragments* (London: Longmans, Green, 1902); and Gertrude Toynbee, ed., *Reminiscences and Letters of Joseph and Arnold Toynbee* (London: H. J. Glaisher, 1910). Toynbee makes some remarks on his uncle in *Acquaintances* (London: Oxford University Press, 1967), pp. 20–22, 33–36.

3. A. J. Toynbee, *A Study of History*, 1 (London and New York: Oxford University Press, 1934), viii.

4. Ibid., p. 339. The list of "Acknowledgements and Thanks" at the conclusion of the *Study* includes a great-uncle, Capt. Henry Toynbee (1819–1909), along with other influences (vol. 10, 1954, 213–42). Toynbee also has an appreciation of the sea-going Captain Henry in *Acquaintances*.

5. A. J. Toynbee, *The Western Question in Greece and Turkey* (Boston: Houghton Mifflin, 1922), p. viii. (Rpt. Howard Fertig, 1968.)

6. *Civilization on Trial* (London: Oxford University Press, 1948), p. 7. Most of Toynbee's stories are told in more than one place; I have not normally cited all the references. In addition to *Acquaintances* and *Experiences*, vol. 10 of *A Study of History* and also portions of *Reconsiderations* should be consulted by the student of Toynbee's autobiographical statements.

7. In addition to the Blue Book, see his *Armenian Atrocities: The Murder of a Nation* (London: Hodder and Stoughton, 1915); *The Destruction of Poland* (London: T. F. Unwin, 1916); *The Belgian Deportations* (London: T. F. Unwin, 1917); *The German Terror in Belgium* (London: Hodder and Stoughton, 1917); and *The German Terror in France* (London: Hodder and Stoughton, 1917).

8. Llewellyn Woodward, *Great Britain and the War of 1914–1918* (London: Methuen, 1967), p. 210, n. 2.

9. *The New Europe* (London: J. M. Dent, 1915), p. 32.

10. *Nationality and the War* (London: J. M. Dent, 1915), p. 499. In some degree Toynbee entered into the discussion of the League of Nations idea at this time. In the records of the American "Inquiry" (National Archives, Department of State files, The Inquiry, Document 992), there is memorandum of a conference with J. W. Headlam and A. J. Toymbee [*sic*], April 30, 1918, on this subject.

11. For some light on Toynbee's experience at Paris, which obviously was an unpleasant one, see portions of his book *Acquaintances*, including the chapters on T. E. Lawrence, W. I. Westermann, and Charles R. Crane; also *Experiences*, pp. 49–60.

12. *The Nation* (London), 34, January 12, 1924, 534.

13. *The Western Question in Greece and Turkey*, p. 362.

14. They were resumed after the war. Toynbee edited, and wrote sections of some of the ten volumes in the series on World War 2 (1939–46) which were published between 1952 and 1958. Since 1946 the annual *Surveys* have been carried on under other editors.

15. Review of 1924 volumes in *London Times Literary Supplement*, March 25, 1926. See also B. E. Schmitt in *American Historical Review*, 31 (January 1926), 328 ff. among other reviews.

16. *Survey of International Affairs*, 1926 (London: Humphrey Milford and Oxford University Press, 1928), p. 228.

17. *Survey*, 1933 (pub. 1934), pp. 120–21.

18. *Survey*, 1935 (pub. 1936), 2:449–50. Some criticized the 1935 and 1936 *Surveys* for departing from objectivity in the handling of the Italian invasion of Ethiopia, where Toynbee scarcely disguised his anti-Italian feelings.

19. "After Munich: The World Outlook," *International Affairs*, 18 (January 1939), 18–19.

20. *Experiences*, p. 101.

21. R. W. Livingstone, ed., *The Legacy of Greece* (Oxford: Clarendon Press, 1921); *Greek Historical Thought from Homer to the Age of Heraclius* (London: J. M. Dent, 1924); and *Greek Civilization and Character: The Self-Revelation of Ancient Greek Society* (London: J. M. Dent, 1924). The latter two were both reprinted in paperback by Mentor and are still available. The "Legacy" series also long remained popular.

22. See Toynbee's remarks on his classical or Renaissance education and its significance for his work in vol. 10 of *A Study of History*, pp. 93–98, and *Reconsiderations*, pp. 575–93.

23. In *Experiences*, p. 101, he says that originally he thought of writing the study "in the form of a commentary on the second chorus in Sophocles' *Antigone*." R. G. Collingwood, in *The Idea of History* (Oxford: Clarendon Press, 1946), p. 74, notes that the Greeks denied inevitability,

feeling that "The person who is about to become involved in a tragedy is actually overwhelmed by it only because he is too blind to see his danger. If he saw it, he could guard against it." The resemblance to Toynbee's major conclusion in A *Study of History* is worth noting.

24. Nevill Forbes, A. J. Toynbee, D. Mitrany, and D. G. Hogarth, *The Balkans: A History of Bulgaria, Serbia, Greece, Rumania and Turkey* (Oxford: Clarendon Press, 1915); A. J. Toynbee and Kenneth P. Kirkwood, *Turkey* (London: E. Benn, 1926, and New York: Scribner's, 1927). The latter book seems to reveal a more pro-Western bias than we associate with Toynbee elsewhere. "The ideals of Western civilization are permeating the country and gradually converting it from an Oriental community, depressed by the weight of Islamic laws and customs and the incubus of superstitution, into a Westernized community enlightened in its outlook and progressive in its attitude" (p. 236). Perhaps Mr. Kirkwood wrote this.

25. The importance he attached to travel may be judged from a remark in *Reconsiderations* (p. 2), that between 1954 and 1960 "I have made good a few of the innumerable gaps in my own knowledge, mainly by travelling around the World and seeing, at first hand, a number of countries that I had previously known only from maps and descriptions." See his *East to West* (London: Oxford University Press, 1958), and later travel books. Admiration for the hardy traveler is a leading Toynbee trait.

26. A. J. Toynbee, A *Study of History*, 2nd ed. (1934; London and New York: Oxford University Press, 1935), 1:11.

27. Ibid., p. 131, for the classification.

28. Marxists, who generally reject him, have found this aspect of Toynbee congenial. Cf. Lucien Goldmann, in Raymond Aron, ed., *L'histoire et ses interpretations* (Paris: Mouton, 1961), p. 77.

29. Quoted by Toynbee in A *Study of History*, 3 (London and New York: Oxford University Press, 1934), 231; from Bergson's *Les deux sources de la Morale et de la Religion* (Paris: Alcan, 1932), p. 181. Bergson's mighty influence was on the 1890–1914 generation, the period during which Toynbee's mind was presumably shaped. Certainly the French philosopher was well known in England then.

But Toynbee tends to cite this late work of Bergson to the exclusion of the greater ones of Bergson's zenith. At one point he calls it Bergson's greatest book. We may infer from this a distinct lack of taste and aptitude for philosophy in the stricter sense, which is certainly a characteristic of Toynbee's essentially empirical and practical mind.

30. The point was neatly put, and Toynbee's whole enormous work rather well summed up, by a Canadian versifier, Geoffrey Vivien, in *Canadian Forum*, 27 (October 1947), p. 156:

> He laid the patient on the bed
> You would have thought that she was dead.
> Eighteen such cases had been known
> And all but four were dead and gone.
> Yet under his dissecting knife
> Appeared some sign of lingering life.
> She looks so fair, so sensitive!
> Has she not still a chance to live?
> He sighed and gravely shook his head.
> "All you can do is pray," he said.

31. Pieter Geyl criticizes the *Hitler's Europe* volume (*Encounters in History* [Meridian Books, 1961], pp. 262 ff.) on the grounds of inadequate knowledge of Continental scholarship. Some of these volumes obviously suffered from coming too soon; and, unlike the earlier *Surveys of International Affairs* volumes of the '20s and '30s, they also came too late; too soon for definitive scholarship, too late for current-use value.

32. Abridgement of vols. 1–6 (London and New York: Oxford University Press, 1947); abridgement of vols. 7–10, together with a summary of the whole (London and New York: Oxford University Press, 1957).

33. *Experiences*, p. 73.

34. *Civilization on Trial* (London: Oxford University Press, 1948), p. 94.

35. *Spectator*, May 12, 1961, p. 685.

36. For one thing, he joins Spengler—though for rather different reasons—in holding that decline set in with the Renaissance, the Middle Ages having been the creative zenith.

37. To Toynbee the besetting sin of the modern Western

world, of course, is the "idolatry" of merely human things and especially of Power, the State.

38. See Toynbee's account in *Acquaintances* (chap. 6) of his long friendship with Namier, marred by some quarrels over Zionism, and of his belief that, in their very different ways, he and Sir Lewis were both trying to break new ground (p. 76).

39. Toynbee paid tribute to the medieval (fourteenth century) Islamic historian by saying flatly that Ibn Khaldun's *Muqqadamat* or Prolegomena to his "Universal History" is the greatest thing of its kind ever written. It is easy to agree with this opinion.

40. As early as 1921, in a chapter on Greek history in *The Legacy of Greece*, Toynbee declared that "The great poets of Greece are of as much assistance in understanding the mental history of Greece (which is after all the essential element in any history) as the philosophers and historians." The use of poetry, fiction, and mythology both as materials of history and as a source of fruitful hypotheses is defended in an Annex to *Study* 1 (pp. 441–64).

41. Though he does not mention this, he might have picked up "withdrawal and return" from Matthew Arnold; see his *Culture and Anarchy* (1869).

2 — The Criticism of Toynbee's History

1. For a striking comment on Toynbee's view from above, see William H. McNeill, in Edward T. Gargan, ed., *The Intent of Toynbee's History* (Chicago: Loyola University Press, 1961), pp. 30–32.

2. R. G. Collingwood, *The Idea of History* (Oxford: Clarendon Press, 1946), pp. 159–65.

3. Hans Kohn, rev. of *A Study of History*, *Nation*, 150, February 17, 1940, 256–57.

4. Richard Chase, "The Historian as Artist," *American Scholar* (Summer 1947), p. 281.

5. James Feibleman, "Toynbee's Theory of History," *Southern Review*, 5 (1940), 690–99.

6. H. Stuart Hughes, rev. of *Reconsiderations*, *New York Herald-Tribune Books*, July 23, 1961, p. 4.

7. Richard E. Sullivan, "Toynbee's Debtors," *South Atlantic Quarterly*, 58, no. 1 (1959), 77–90. Edward T. Fox,

"History and Mr. Toynbee," *Virginia Quarterly Review*, 36 (1960), 458–63: "Mr. Toynbee, as an historian, rises above both his critics and his own ponderous work. . . . Right or wrong, good or bad, the Study has been recognized . . . as a major work." McNeill, in Gargan, *Intent of Toynbee's History*, p. 30: "Even if all but a few fragments of Toynbee's text should prove vulnerable to attack on the grounds of factual inaccuracy, still the book would stand . . . as a notable monument of our century's intellectual history."

8. Geoffrey Barraclough, in *The Listener*, 52, October 14, 1954, 639; reprinted in M. F. Ashley Montagu, ed., *Toynbee and History* (Boston: Porter Sargent, 1956), pp. 118–21.

9. See Ashley Montagu, *Toynbee and History* and Gargan, *Intent of Toynbee's History*; also Raymond Aron, ed., *L'histoire et ses interpretations: entretiens autour de Arnold Toynbee* (Paris: Mouton, 1961). A great deal of Toynbee commentary is also summarized in Henry L. Mason, *Toynbee's Approach to World Politics* (New Orleans: Tulane University Press, 1958).

10. For Geyl's war with Toynbee see Pieter Geyl, *Debates with Historians* (New York: Meridian Books, 1958), which contains four essays on Toynbee; also some passages in his *Encounters in History* (New York: Meridian Books, 1961), e.g., pp. 328–30.

11. It should be noted that Toynbee submitted parts of his work to other scholars for criticism while he was writing *A Study of History*, and that he printed their comments in the body of his work. Examples of this are: G. F. Hudson's remarks on Nomadic eruptions (3:453 ff.); critical comment by Geoffrey Barraclough throughout the portions of vol. 4 on the post-Hildebrandine medieval papacy (4:520, 526, 533, 539, 548, 550, 577); criticism by Gilbert Murray of the handling of Stoicism (6:154); many comments by Martin Wight on Christianity and the Church in vol. 7 (see Toynbee's explanation in 10:738); and many others. The criticism did not often seem to change Toynbee's view but he printed it for the reader's benefit.

The unfailing courtesy with which Toynbee has given as well as received criticism, often in the teeth of rather strong provocation, stamps him as a true practicer of the charity he has recommended in his writings.

12. See vol. 4, *A Study of History* (London and New

York: Oxford University Press, 1939), p. 290. The name of Wilson was removed (rather conspicuously, in my copy) from later printings. Oscar Handlin, in his unfriendly "In the Dark Backward," *Partisan Review*, 14 (1947), 371–79, noted that Toynbee still had not corrected the error, but he did so some time thereafter. The Charles A. Beard review was in *American Historical Review* (April 1940), p. 594.

13. In *The World and the West* (London: Oxford University Press, 1953), pp. 12–13, Toynbee says that communism was the first "creed" that Russia ever borrowed from the West. What he means by "creed" is uncertain; but Russians had borrowed the ideology of the *philosophes* in the eighteenth century, romanticism and Hegelianism and positivism (among others) in the nineteenth. These doctrines powerfully influenced the Russian intelligentsia. They had at least as much impact as Marxism until the latter happened to profit by the disaster of World War I.

14. Barraclough, *The Listener*, p. 639. See also criticisms of Toynbee's theses about Russia expressed in *The World and the West*, ibid., 48 (November 27, 1952), 893–94.

15. J. Clarkson, "Toynbee on Slavic and Russian History," *Russian Review*, 15, no. 3 (July 1956); H. Stammler, "Russia between Byzantium and Utopia," ibid., 17, no. 7 (April 1958); Hans Kohn, "Toynbee and Russia," in Gargan, *Intent of Toynbee's History*—the latter less critical than the others. Cf. Toynbee's replies to these criticisms in *Reconsiderations: A Study of History*, 12 (London, New York, Toronto: Oxford University Press, 1961), 536–46.

16. Raymond Dawson, *The Chinese Chameleon: An Analysis of European Conceptions of Chinese Civilization* (London: Oxford University Press, 1967) pp. 85–88. He makes much the same points as Wayne Altree, "Toynbee and Chinese History," in Ashley Montagu, *Toynbee and History*, who similarly finds that "the facts of Chinese history do not square with Toynbee's theory." Most historians of China do not discuss Toynbee at all. Joseph Needham, *Science and Civilization in China*, 1 (Cambridge: Cambridge University Press, 1954), p. 241, refers to Toynbee's view (*Study of History*, 3:386) that the Chinese had a religious and esthetic but not a mechanical talent as an example of a quaint delusion of occidentals. Victor Purcell once was moved to write a satire on Toynbee. Cf. the rather gentler articles of Meribeth Cameron, "A Bisection of Chi-

nese History," *Pacific Historical Review*, 8 (December 1939), 401–12, and "A Rehandling of Japanese History," *Far Eastern Quarterly*, 1 (February 1942), 150–60.

17. These scattered citations must not be taken for anything like a full listing of Toynbee criticism, which would probably require a volume in itself. Milton Gold has written on "Toynbee and the Turks" in *Journal of the Royal Society of Great Britain and Ireland* (1961), pp. 77–99. For a note on Toynbee's misconception of Sudanese Mahdism, see letters by S. Hilleson and E. Atiyah in *The Listener*, January 1 and 8, 1953.

18. C. E. von Grunebaum, "Toynbee's Conception of Islamic History," in Gargan, *Intent of Toynbee's History*; the same historian's *Der Islam in Seiner Klassischen Epoche 622–1258* (Zurich and Stuttgart: Artemis Verlag, 1963), p. 176. Rushton Coulborn, in Ashley Montagu, *Toynbee and History*, a generally sympathetic critic, is also "left gasping" by Toynbee's "preposterous" classifications of Syriac and Islamic civilizations. N. Bammate, in Aron, *L'histoire*, p. 198, pays tribute, from a Middle Eastern perspective, to Toynbee's enlargement of history to embrace other peoples.

19. L. Renou, "The Civilization of India according to Arnold Toynbee," *Diogenes* (Spring 1956), pp. 69–80, is only partly critical. O. H. K. Spate, in his *India and Pakistan* (London: Methuen, 1954), p. 158 n., praises Toynbee's "very penetrating analysis" of geographic and economic factors in Indian history. For the adoption of a Toynbee concept, see Percival Spear, *India: A Modern History* (Ann Arbor: University of Michigan Press, 1961), p. 174.

20. For Toynbee's rejoinders to these attacks see *Reconsiderations*, pp. 293–300, 604–16, 627–28. So sympathetic a critic as Lewis Mumford called his handling of the Jews his "major lapse." Were the Black Nationalists to turn their attention to Toynbee, one shudders at what might be the results, for he did not think black Africa had yet produced a civilization, though he thought its peoples had the capability to do so; see *A Study of History*, 1 (London and New York: Oxford University Press, 1934), 233 ff.

21. See James T. Shotwell, *At the Paris Peace Conference* (New York: Macmillan, 1937), p. 75; a number of other eyewitnesses are referred to in Lawrence E. Gelfand, *The Inquiry; American Preparations for Peace 1917–1919* (New Haven: Yale University Press, 1963), pp. 170–74.

Toynbee is also quite in error in stating (*Acquaintances* [London: Oxford University Press, 1967], p. 175) that George Bernard Shaw did not write plays until after he was married.

It sometimes seems that it is almost impossible to read a page of Toynbee without coming across some annoying little error of this sort. One more example only: vol. 3 (*A Study of History* [London and New York: Oxford University Press, 1934]), p. 304, where in the midst of a fascinating and well-written discussion of the rise of peripheral states to upset an old balance of power, he uses Canning's phrase "call in a new world to redress the balance of the old" and, in a footnote, explains its occasion quite wrongly. Canning did not use this famous expression "in allusion to the part which British statesmanship had played in the liberation of a score of new nations . . . in South and Central America," but in allusion to his *detente* and joint action with the United States in fending off a supposed threat by the continental Holy Alliance powers to intervene in Latin America.

22. E. Atiyah, in *The Listener*, 49, January 1, 1953, 26. Cf. Collingwood, "really a scheme of pigeon holes elaborately arranged and labelled, into which ready made historical facts can be put" (*The Idea of History*, p. 163).

23. *Reconsiderations*, pp. 13–19.

24. Toynbee at times has said that he prefers "regularities" to "laws" (which he usually puts in quotation marks) since "it is doubtful if the regularities have the same rigor as in the biological and especially the mechanical domain" (Aron, *L'histoire*, pp. 196–97). In *Reconsiderations*, however, he argues not only that he has discovered "genuine regularities and reoccurrences in the configuration of past events" but that these are quite as valid as generalizations about physical bodies (pp. 239–40). In a letter to Kenneth W. Thompson, quoted by the latter in his article "Toynbee and International Politics," *Political Science Quarterly*, 71 (1956), 368, Toynbee wrote that "As to the issue between recurrence and uniqueness, I think both elements are present in history as in everything else, and the logical difficulty of reconciling them is neither greater nor smaller in history than in other fields of thought." Throughout his *A Study of History*, and elsewhere, Toynbee has in fact assumed that he is engaged in discovering laws or regularities or reoccur-

rences which have a high degree of validity and may be regarded as comparable to the laws discovered by the other sciences.

25. Karl R. Popper, *The Poverty of Historicism* (Boston: Beacon Press, 1957), epigraph, v, et passim. On pp. 110–11 Popper associates Toynbee with a Platonic great-cycle theory intuitively arrived at which then searches out facts to support it, ignoring other facts that do not. Cf. also Isaiah Berlin, *Historical Inevitability* (London: Oxford University Press, 1955), pp. 69–74.

26. W. H. Walsh, *An Introduction to Philosophy of History* (London: Hutchinson, 1951), p. 47.

27. Raymond Aron, *Main Currents of Sociological Thought*, 2 (New York: Basic Books, 1967), viii. Cf. G. Duncan Mitchell, *A Hundred Years of Sociology* (1968), p. 245, for similar remarks.

28. See Irving Goldman, "Evolution and Anthropology," *Victorian Studies*, 3 (September 1959), pp. 55–75; Robert L. Carneiro, introduction to *The Evolution of Society: Selections from Herbert Spencer's Principles of Sociology* (Chicago: University of Chicago Press, 1967). The large reputation today of Claude Lévi-Strauss would seem to rest on his formulation of challenging (however dubious) generalizations, by a scholar who, like Toynbee, is an apparent master (*trés formidable*) of the enormous empirical data accumulated by workaday anthropologists; but Lévi-Strauss, like Toynbee, is unique.

29. P. J. Allen, ed., *Pitirim A. Sorokin in Review* (Durham: Duke University Press, 1963).

30. The philosopher William Dray, "Toynbee's Search for Historical Laws," *History and Theory*, 1, no. 1 (1960), 32–54, and the sociologist Jean Floud, writing in the same journal, vol. 4 (1965), 271–75, are among those who find Toynbee's program acceptable in principle but a failure in practice, because attempted on far too large a scale. The more extreme criticism may be seen in Alan Donagan's rejection (ibid., 4:25) of those who would "mutilate research into human affairs by remodelling the social sciences into deformed likenesses of physics."

31. Edward P. Cheyney, "Law in History," *American Historical Review*, 29 (January 1924), pp. 231–48.

32. Such is the burden of a hundred complaints; yet the

phrase has stuck, and for an opinion that Challenge-and-Response is sociologically sound, see Michael P. Fogarty, "The Rhythm of Change," *Review of Politics*, 22 (1960), 451–65.

33. For example, by W. H. Walsh in "Toynbee Reconsidered," *Philosophy*, 38 (1963), 77. I do not think Walsh is right when he adds that Toynbee is not really seeking explanations of historical change, but only regularities. Toynbee is keenly interested in explanations, but he is too good an historian to be able to find any mechanical ones, and so he is driven to very generalized and vaguely metaphorical ones.

34. See, for example, Norman H. Baynes and R. St. L. B. Moss, eds., *Byzantium: An Introduction to East Roman Civilization* (Oxford: Clarendon Press, 1948), pp. xv–xx, where these eminent Byzantinists oppose Toynbee's view that there was a break and a new civilization, as well as the view that Leo III's absolutism was a fatal error. Byzantine specialists also deny that the Church was uniformly subservient to the State, despite the formal union of powers; cf. E. A. Stephanou, "Toynbee and the Orthodox Christian Society," *Greek Orthodox Theological Review*, 2 (1956), 27–40, and E. R. Hardy, in Gargan, *Intent of Toynbee's History*, pp. 163–64.

35. See, for example, José Ferrater Mora, *Man at the Crossroads* (Boston: Beacon Presg, 1957), and José Ortega y Gasset, *Man and Crisis* (London: George Allen & Unwin, 1959), both of which see many parallels between the ancient world and that of modern Europe. So did perhaps the first great pessimistic historian of the contemporary epoch, Jacob Burckhardt.

36. Karl Jaspers, *Man in the Modern Age* (London: Routledge and Kegan Paul, 1951), p. 21

37. V. Gordon Childe, *History* (London: Cobbett Press, 1947), p. 63; cited by W. Den Boer in Ashley Montagu, *Toynbee and History*, p. 225.

38. The point is made by Grunebaum in Gargan, *Intent of Toynbee's History*, p. 108.

39. Criticism of Toynbee's handling of Greek and Roman history has been abundant; see, for example, the essays by W. Den Boer in Ashley Montagu, and David M. Robinson in Gargan; also J. Vogt, "Die Antike Kultur in Toynbee's

Geschichtlehre," *Saeculum,* 2 (1951), 557–74. Toynbee perhaps misses the point in placing the argument on the meaningless grounds of whether to classify the era of the Roman state as Hellenic or Roman. What his critics have often accused him of is belittling Rome's achievement. See, for example, Norman R. Baynes, *Byzantine Studies and Other Essays* (London: Athlone Press, 1960), p. 73.

40. "For the historian . . . the past is feminine. He loves it as a mistress of whom he never tires, and whom he never expects to talk sense." Michael Oakeshott, "The Activity of Being an Historian," in *Historical Studies: Papers Read before the Second Irish Conference of Historians* (London: Bowes & Bowes, 1958), p. 19.

The compulsion to find perfect regularities reaches a fever point, bordering on sheer insanity, in vol. 9 (*Study of History,* pp. 234–87) when Toynbee, juggling figures and concepts madly, tries to show that there is an exact cycle of wars in the last stages of a disintegrating civilization. (This is in line with the extremely dubious theory that determinism takes over ever more as the end approaches: in youth civilizations are relatively free, in old age they are bound by necessity. Could not one just as plausibly argue the opposite, noting that declining societies tend to "lose control" and behave with unpredictable irrationality?) To no historian could these charts plotting cycles of wars have any possible meaning. The idea that wars come, not because of specific circumstances at a given time that may be analyzed, but because of some time-cycle that decrees they will come at a certain moment and no other, smacks of astrological mysticism more than science and is surely the nadir of Toynbee's method.

41. In Aron, *L'histoire,* p. 49. Cf. Raymond Aron in his *Eighteen Lectures on Industrial Society* (London: Weidenfeld and Nicolson, 1967), p. 27: "Insofar as social theories claim to present an exact, authentic and universally valid reproduction of social structures they cease to be scientific."

42. José Ortega y Gasset, *Man and Crisis,* p. 13.

3—Toynbee's Mind and Art

1. Morris Watnick, "Toynbee's Nine Books of History against the Pagans," *Antioch Review,* 7 (1947), 607.

2. O. H. K. Spate, *"Finis Coronat Opus?"* Australian Outlook, 16, no. 1 (1962), 84–89.

3. Bruce Mazlish, *The Riddle of History: The Great Speculators from Vico to Freud* (New York: Harper & Row, 1966), p. 377.

4. Oscar Handlin, "In the Dark Backward," *Partisan Review*, 14 (1947), 378–79. For another objection that Toynbee is "not democratic," Marie C. Swabey, *The Judgment of History* (New York: Philosophical Library, 1954), p. 222.

5. H. R. Trevor-Roper, "Arnold Toynbee's Millennium," *Encounter*, 45 (1957), 14–28, reprinted in his *Historical Essays* (New York: Harper & Row, Torchbooks, 1966). Cf. A. J. P. Taylor's sneers in M. F. Ashley Montagu, ed., *Toynbee and History* (Boston: Porter Sargent, 1956).

6. Reprinted in Richard H. S. Crossman, *The Charm of Politics* (New York: Harper, 1958), p. 96.

7. In *The Open Society and Its Enemies,* 4th ed. rev. (London: Routledge and Kegan Paul, 1962), 2:251 ff., Karl Popper accuses Toynbee of "irrationality" and makes it the burden of his charge that Toynbee does not take arguments "seriously, and at their face value," but rather sees in them "nothing but a way in which deeper irrational motives and tendencies express themselves." He means by this that Toynbee typically sees ideas and philosophies as reflecting a certain stage in historical development. This is quite true, as it is also true and must be true of any naturalistic study of society. Ideas are a part of the natural order and must be at least partly explained by the social situation or (Spengler) the stage of development in which a civilization finds itself. As we know, Toynbee believed religions and philosophies to be the soul's reflection of the civilization's growth stage: Stoicism and Buddhism appeared during breakdown and disintegration, etc. Is this irrationalism? If so, virtually all historians and sociologists would appear to be guilty in the same way. They need not hold that this is the *only* level on which ideas have meaning (reductionism), and it seems clear that Toynbee does not so hold. For example, he clearly thinks Stoicism must be evaluated on its merits as a moral philosophy since he examines and criticizes it as such. In any case, Toynbee is seeking a rational explanation of beliefs, in the sense that he would regard them as explicable and comprehensible from social analysis.

8. In a critical analysis of Toynbee's influence on Middle

Eastern policy, via the Royal Institute, Elie Kedourie noted especially the "simple certainties and draconian verdicts," the moralism and rhetoric—to which he attributed an unfortunate influence on British policies. See "The Chatham House Version," in Kedourie's *The Chatham House Version and Other Middle-Eastern Studies* (New York: Praeger, 1970).

9. This advice, which Toynbee often repeated, may be found in his *The Present-Day Experiment in Western Civilization* (London: Oxford University Press, 1962).

10. *The Judgment of History*, p. 223. See Toynbee's *Civilization on Trial* (London: Oxford University Press, 1948) and *An Historian's Approach to Religion* (London: Oxford University Press, 1956) for such views.

11. Toynbee has scolded the Church for opposing the march of Western science from the seventeenth century on, considerably exaggerating the degree to which it did so, rather in the spirit of Thomas Huxley's baiting of ecclesiasticals—see vol. 7 (*A Study of History*, 1954), 465–83. He is prepared, like Huxley, to ask religion to surrender all "intellectual knowledge" to science.

12. November 27, 1952; see also correspondence in subsequent issues of *The Listener*, through January 1, 1953. The debate in the columns of the *Times Literary Supplement* upon review of the book was published by the London *Times* as *The Toynbee–Jerrold Controversy: Letters to the Editor of the Times Literary Supplement* (1954).

13. In an interview published in *Christian Century* in 1950 (R. M. Bartlett, "Toynbee on Korea," 67, pp. 946–47), he was quoted as saying that "The U.N. has at last made a wise step in taking a stand against Communism . . . communistic aggression," and "if we fail to work together now, the Communists of Russia will enslave us."

14. "If I had to make the terrible choice of being conquered by a nationalist Germany and being conquered by the Communist Russia, I myself would opt for Russian Communism as against German nationalism." (A. J. Toynbee, *America and the World Revolution* [London: Oxford University Press, 1962], p. 96.) Or as against American nationalism, which seems a more likely choice? He blames the United States for being hostile to Soviet Russia (ibid., p. 97).

15. John Wendon, "Christianity, History, and Mr. Toyn-

bee," *Journal of Religion*, 36 (1956), 139–49. Numerous other Christian theologians have made the same point; as, for example, A. Messineo, "Le Storicismo Progressista," in *Civilta Catholica*, 107 (1956), 239–51; and Father F. G. Klenk, in *Stimmen der Zeit*, 166, no. 8 (1960), 148–52.

16. Perhaps one should write "yesterday's." The domination which the school of Barth, Bultmann, and Tillich exercised over European theology from 1920 until the present has been challenged recently by a more historical-minded school, associated with Prof. W. Pannenberg of Mainz. But a scrutiny of such recent books as James M. Robinson and John B. Cobb, eds., *Theology as History* (New York: Harper & Row, 1967), V. A. Harvey, *The Historian and the Believer* (New York: Macmillan, 1966), and Carl E. Braaten, *History and Hermeneutics* (Philadelphia: Westminster Press, 1966) yields, alas, no single mention of Toynbee. Toynbee is not, it should be noted, an historical Christian in the sense of defending the facticity of the Gospel story; in a quite literal-minded way he denies the literal truth of the Virgin birth, miracles, and ascension of Christ.

17. Sidney Hook, "Mr. Toynbee's City of God," *Partisan Review*, 15, no. 6 (June 1948). In a similar way, *The Listener* editorially wondered whether one could not succumb to despair about the modern world without the need for all that history (vol. 52, October 14, 1954, 606).

18. "What World War II Did and Didn't Settle," *New York Times Magazine*, May 1, 1955. Toynbee also suggested that the world religions correspond to Jung's psychological types, Christianity being extravert-feeling, Islam extravert-sensing, Hinduism introvert-thinking, Buddhism introvert-intuiting. In the future world order each might attract its congenial personality type in all countries. See *A Study of History*, 7:716–36.

19. This similarity is detected by Gwilym O. Griffith in his "Professor Toynbee, Mazzini, and the Future Faith," *Hibbert Journal*, 54 (1956), 221–25. A writer who finds Toynbee's religious descriptions good but his outlook naïve is Jean Pepin, "La religion d'un historien," *Mercure de France*, no. 1208 (1964), pp. 301–11.

20. A book with the same title as Wagar's, *The City of Man* (New York: Viking Press, 1940) was issued as a "declaration on world democracy" by a group of American and European refugee intellectuals including such names as

Borgese, Van Wyck Brooks, Thomas Mann, Mumford, Reinhold Niebuhr, and Gaetano Salvemini. It called for "the Nation of Man embodied in the Universal State, the State of States" (p. 74), and, repudiating "the heresy of nationalism," predicted "a Universal Parliament" and a "President of Mankind—no crowned emperor, no hereditary king." It abjured revolution, "an obsessive myth of the modern mind in its decay," and proposed a nonsectarian Christian spirit as a "universal religion" (pp. 35–36). Though some of the authors demonstrably knew Toynbee well (Mumford, Hans Kohn), he is not quoted and it seems more likely that this idea was simply "in the air" as the Second World War dawned; it was here given a typically American version marked by optimism and of course democracy.

21. Helen P. Leibel has written an interesting article on "The Historian and the Idea of World Civilization," in *Dalhousie Review*, 47 (1968), 455–66.

22. *An Historian's Approach to Religion*, p. 218. "The reason why the League failed [to prevent World War II]," Toynbee wrote in *The World in March 1939* (London: Oxford University Press, 1952), "was that the enforcement of the Covenant had been backed by insufficient armed power and insufficient resolution to use such power as was available." The league, as such, possessed no power except what its leading members might choose to give to it; it was not an agent with a will of its own, but only a meeting place of the sovereign Powers. It had not been intended as a balance-of-power device, but as an entirely different system, that of "collective security." But in fact this thinking was muddled and collective security failed to provide an adequate substitute for the familiar balance-of-power and diplomacy order, and this is still the case.

23. Arnold J. Toynbee, *America and the World Revolution and Other Lectures* (London: Oxford University Press, 1962) p. 67. Here he decides that the best bet for a world dictator would be an avatar of Gandhi, perhaps a Buddhist or Hindu sage (pp. 72–74).

24. Toynbee himself, looking at the African and Arab worlds in *Between Niger and Nile* (London: Oxford University Press, 1965), found that in neither of these societies did the cause of unity look hopeful, while tension and not harmony marked relations between them (p. 124).

25. Indian religious exercises have become very modish in

the West, as is well known; but they have flourished among the alienated, as a gesture of rejection of the Western civilization including Christianity, and this militates against any synthesis. For a description of a California cult purporting to combine Christianity and Buddhism, but which in fact seems almost exclusively Buddhist or pseudo-Buddhist (the Self Realization Fellowship), see Orrin E. Klapp, *Collective Search for Identity* (New York: Holt, Rinehart and Winston), pp. 165–67.

26. The ferment in Africa is suggested by David B. Barrett's recent book, *Schism and Renewal in Africa* (London: Oxford University Press, 1969), which examines no fewer than six thousand contemporary religious movements within the Protestant and Catholic churches there.

27. Ninian Smart, *The Religious Experience of Mankind* (New York: Charles Scribner's Sons, 1968), pp. 526, 537. It might be noted that a syncretic religious movement, such as Baha'i from Islam or Ramakrishna Vedanta from India, tends to become just another sect competing for followers. In an incorrigibly pluralistic society those who call for unity only add additional voices to the bedlam.

28. *Historian's Approach to Religion*, p. 216.

29. Mircea Eliade, *From the Primitive to Zen: A Thematic Sourcebook of the History of Religions* (New York: Harper & Row, 1967); see also his *Myths, Dreams and Mysteries* (New York: Harper & Row, Torchbooks, 1963) and other books.

30. Eric Roth, "A Theologian Looks at Professor Toynbee's Philosophy of History," *Hibbert Journal*, 44 (1956) 213–20.

31. Pitirim Sorokin, rev. of *Study of History* in *Journal of Modern History*, 12 (1940), 379; Walter Kaufmann, "The Historian as False Prophet," *Commentary*, 23 (1957), 348; E. F. J. Zahn, *Toynbee und das Problem der Geschichte* (Cologne: Westdeutscher Verlag, 1954), p. 37.

32. R. H. Tawney, "Dr. Toynbee's Study of History," *International Affairs*, 18 (November 1939), 798–806. Cf. H. A. L. Fisher, *Pages from the Past* (Oxford: Clarendon Press, 1939), p. 727: "Wherever he ranges—and he goes everywhere—he has something to say which is fresh and arresting."

33. Jürgen von Kempski, "Stilisierte Geschichte," *Welt als Geschichte*, 21 (1961), 131–57.

34. James Feibleman, "Toynbee's Theory of History," *Southern Review*, 5 (1940), 699.

35. John T. Marcus, *Heaven, Hell and History* (New York and London: Macmillan, 1967), p. 271.

36. Den Boer, in Ashley Montagu, *Toynbee and History*, p. 242.

37. Glenn Tinder, "The Necessity of Historicism," *American Political Science Review*, 55 (September 1961), pp. 560–65.

38. *History and Theory*, vol. 4 (1964), p. 129, rev. by AJT of book by Kroeber and Kluckhohn.

39. A recent article by Professor Theodore H. Von Laue, asking "Is There a Crisis in the Writing of History?" (*Bucknell Review*, 14 [1966], 1–15), makes the point that contemporary specialist history fails to serve the public need for knowledge and guidance. The same message has been repeated in articles and books too numerous to mention. The sense of a crisis has led to all kinds of proposals for change, from quantification to globalization, most of them weirder than anything in Toynbee.

40. Special supplement, "Books in a Changing World," *Times Literary Supplement*, August 15, 1958, pp. xxiv–xxv.

41. "History by Team-work," in A. O. Sarkissian, ed., *Studies in Diplomatic History and Historiography in Honour of G. P. Gooch* (New York: Barnes & Noble, 1962), p. 11.

42. The best known of such attempts is probably William H. McNeill's *The Rise of the West: A History of the Human Community* (Chicago: University of Chicago Press, 1963) of which his *A World History* (London: Oxford University Press, 1967) is substantially a shortened version; McNeill, though he has written sympathetically about Toynbee, announces himself as hostile to "the Spengler-Toynbee view that a number of separate civilizations pursued essentially independent careers" and stresses both cultural diffusion and interrelationships between a small number of cultural areas. He is extremely wary about "laws" though occasionally he suggests one. In practice, the book is not very different from separate histories of the West, the Far East, and the Middle East. It does not suggest any particular *telos* of history but does predict a "world-wide cosmopolitanism" as probable for the future (cf. the same author's *Past and Future* [Chicago: University of Chicago Press, 1954]). The level of thought and quality of expression is a bit

below Toynbee, but as a textbook it has proved useful and is much more "one-world"-ish.

43. John Gross, *The Rise and Fall of the Man of Letters* (London: Weidenfeld and Nicolson, 1969).

44. "Dr. Toynbee's Study of History: A Review," *International affairs*, 31 (1955), 16. Eric Voegelin, in his *Order and History* (3 vols.; Baton Rouge: Louisiana State University Press, 1956–1957) accepts Toynbee's view that civilizations are the only "intelligible units of study" and like Spengler tries to reveal their personalities or forms, but differs from Toynbee in realizing that man can never discover the ultimate meaning of history.

Selected Bibliography

No attempt is made here to list all the works either by or about Toynbee. Each would be a formidable enterprise. The following bibliographies would be useful in any such project, though with obvious gaps: O'Callaghan, Phyllis. "A Selective Bibliography on *A Study of History*." *Historical Bulletin* (London), March 1956, pp. 168–81; Popper, Monica. *A Bibliography of the Works in English of Arnold Toynbee, 1910–1954*. London: Royal Institute of International Affairs, 1955; Rule, John C. and Barbara S. Crosby. "Bibliography of Works about Toynbee in Western Languages, 1946–1960." *History and Theory* 4 (1964), 213–33.

The bibliography given below is largely confined to works mentioned or cited in this book. The list is no more than a fair sampling of the more significant criticisms of Toynbee. Nor is anything like a full listing of Toynbee's own writings included, especially of his articles in magazines and newspapers, which have been numerous, though most of them repeat what he wrote elsewhere and often were included in books. The student interested in running these to earth will find *Historical Abstracts* (1955–) useful, as well as the better-known guides to periodical literature such as *International Index, Reader's Guide to Periodicals,* and *International Bibliographie der Zeitschriftenliteratur*. A bibliography on "Works in the Philosophy of History" has been kept in the journal *History and Theory*; see 1961, 1963, 1967, and presumably the continuations.

Writings by Arnold J. Toynbee

Armenian Atrocities: *The Murder of a Nation*. London: Hodder and Stoughton, 1915.

The Balkans: A History of Bulgaria, Serbia, Greece, Rumania and Turkey. With N. Forbes, D. Mitrany, and D. G. Hogarth. Section on Greece written by Toynbee. Oxford: The Clarendon Press, 1915.

Nationality and the War. London: J. M. Dent, 1915.

The New Europe: Some Essays in Reconstruction. London: J. M. Dent, 1915.

The Treatment of Armenians in the Ottoman Empire 1915–1916. London: His Majesty's Stationery Office, 1916. Edited by AJT; official publication; documents.

The Belgian Deportations. London: Thomas F. Unwin, 1917.

The Destruction of Poland: A Study in German Efficiency. London: Thomas F. Unwin, 1917.

The German Terror in Belgium. London: Hodder and Stoughton, 1917.

The German Terror in France. London: Hodder and Stoughton, 1917.

The Western Question in Greece and Turkey. Boston: Houghton Mifflin Co., 1922.

Greek Civilization and Character: The Self-revelation of Ancient Greek Society. Edited; introduction and translations by AJT. London: J. M. Dent, 1924.

Greek Historical Thought from Homer to the Age of Heraclius. Edited; introduction and translations by AJT. London: J. M. Dent, 1924.

Royal Institute of International Affairs (London) publications, produced under Toynbee's direction and written wholly or in part by him; published by Oxford University Press and Humphrey Milford, London: *Surveys of International Affairs*; first volume 1920–23 and thereafter annually through 1939; *The World After the Peace Conference* (1925); *The Islamic World since the Peace Settlement* (1927); *The Conduct of British Empire Foreign Relations since the Peace Settlement* (1928). *Surveys of International Affairs,* 1939–46. Of the ten volumes in this series on World War II, all written under his direction, only the following contain significant writings by AJT: *The Eve of the War,* 1939 (1958), and *The Initial Triumph of the Axis* (1958). Some of the others contain short introductions by him.

Turkey. With Kenneth P. Kirkwood. London: E. Benn, 1926.

A Journey to China. London: Constable and Co., 1931.

A Study of History. Vols. 1–3, 1934; vols. 4–6, 1939; vols. 7–10, 1954; vol. 11, with Edward D. Myers, *Historical Atlas and Gazeteer*, 1959; vol. 12, *Reconsiderations*, 1961. All published by Oxford University Press, London and New York. Abridgement by D. C. Somervell of vols. 1–6: Oxford University Press, 1947, and vols. 7–10: Oxford University Press, 1957.

Christianity and Civilization. The Burge Memorial Lecture, Oxford, 1940. London: Student Christian Movement Press, 1940.

Civilization on Trial. London: Oxford University Press, 1948.

The World and the West. London: Oxford University Press, 1953.

An Historian's Approach to Religion. London: Oxford University Press, 1956.

Christianity among the Religions of the World. London: Oxford University Press, 1957.

East to West: A Journey round the World. London: Oxford University Press, 1958.

Hellenism: The History of a Civilization. London: Oxford University Press, 1959.

Between Oxus and Jumna. London: Oxford University Press, 1961.

America and the World Revolution and Other Lectures. London: Oxford University Press, 1962.

The Economy of the Western Hemisphere. London: Oxford University Press, 1962.

The Present-Day Experiment in Western Civilization. London: Oxford University Press, 1962.

Between Niger and Nile. London: Oxford University Press, 1965.

Hannibal's Legacy: The Hannibalic War's Effects on Roman Life. London: Oxford University Press, 1965, 2 vols.

Between Maule and Amazon. London: Oxford University Press, 1966.

Change and Habit: The Challenge of Our Time. London: Oxford University Press, 1966.

Acquaintances. London: Oxford University Press, 1967.

Experiences. London: Oxford University Press, 1969.

Cities on the Move. London: Oxford University Press, 1970. Rather modishly antitechnological as well as anti-megalopolitan, the coming one great World City being viewed glumly. Here is further evidence for the quite predictable pattern of Toynbee's social and political thought.

Surviving the Future. London: Oxford University Press, 1971.

ESSAYS AND ARTICLES

"History." In R. W. Livingston, ed., *The Legacy of Greece.* Oxford: Clarendon Press, 1921.

"The Greek Door to the Study of History." In *Essays in Honor of Gilbert Murray.* London: G. Allen and Unwin, 1936.

"After Munich: The World Outlook." *International Affairs* 18 (1939), 1–28.

"A Turning Point in History." *Foreign Affairs* 17 (1939), 305–20.

"The International Outlook." *International Affairs* 26 (1947), 463–76.

Dialogue with Pieter Geyl. In *Can We Know the Pattern of the Past?* Bussum: Kroonder, 1948.

"Can Russia Really Change?" *New York Times Magazine,* July 24, 1955.

"Comment on Geyl's and Fiess's Reviews." *Journal of the History of Ideas* 16, no. 3 (1955). Geyl, "Toynbee the Prophet," and Edward Fiess, "Toynbee as Poet," appeared in the previous issue.

"Toynbee Answers Ten Basic Questions," *New York Times Magazine,* February 20, 1955.

"What World War II Did and Didn't Settle," *New York Times Magazine,* May 1, 1955.

"The Writing of History." In *Times Literary Supplement,* August 15, 1958, special issue, "Books in a Changing World."

"The Future of Religion," *Twentieth Century* 170 (1961), 114–39.

"Jewish Rights in Israel," *Jewish Quarterly Review* 52 (1961), 1–11. Reply by S. Zeitlin in same issue.

"History by Team-work." In A. O. Sarkissian, ed., *Studies in*

Diplomatic History and Historiography in Honour of
G. P. Gooch. New York: Barnes and Noble, 1962.
"Sorokin's Philosophy of History." In Phillip J. Allen, ed.,
Pitirim A. Sorokin in Review. Durham: Duke Uni-
versity Press, 1963.
Review of A. L. Kroeber and Clyde Kluckhohn, *Culture, A*
Critical Review of Concepts and Definitions. History
and Theory 4 (1964), 127–29.

Writings about Toynbee

BOOKS

Aron, Raymond, ed. *L'histoire et ses interprétations: en-*
tretiens autour de Arnold Toynbee. Paris: Mouton,
1961. Only loosely about Toynbee; contains some
remarks by AJT.
Ashley Montagu, M. F., ed. *Toynbee and History.* Boston:
Porter Sargent, 1956. An extensive collection of articles including many of the best criticisms.
Counsels of Hope: The Toynbee-Jerrold Controversy: Let-
ters to the Editor of the Times Literary Supplement,
with Leading Articles. London: The Times Publish-
ing Co., 1954.
Eban, Abba. *The Toynbee Heresy.* New York: Israel In-
formation Office, 1955. Pamphlet; reprinted in Ash-
ley Montagu.
Gargan, Edward T., ed. *The Intent of Toynbee's History.*
Chicago: Loyola University Press, 1961. Uneven
quality but some valuable commentary.
Geyl, Pieter. *Debates with Historians.* Cleveland and New
York: Meridian Books, 1958. Contains four essays
on Toynbee.
Jerrold, Douglas. *The Lie about the West.* London: J. M.
Dent, 1954.
Martin, Percival W. *Experiment in Depth: A Study of the*
Work of Jung, Eliot, Toynbee. London: Routledge
and Kegan Paul, 1955.
Mason, Henry L. *Toynbee's Approach to World Politics.*
Tulane Studies in Political Science, vol. 5. New Or-
leans: Tulane University Press, 1958. A useful biblio-
graphy of Toynbee criticisms is on pp. 147–51.

Samuel, Maurice. *The Professor and the Fossil*. New York: A. Knopf, 1956.

Zahn, E. F. J. *Toynbee und das Problem der Geschichte*. Cologne: Westdeutscher Verlag, 1954.

SPECIFIC PASSAGES IN BOOKS

Berlin, Isaiah. *Historical Inevitability*. London: Oxford University Press, 1955.

Beus, J. G. de. *The Future of the West*. New York: Harper, 1953. Belongs among the defenders of the West against Spenglerian and Toynbeean pessimism.

Collingwood, R. G. *The Idea of History*. Oxford: Clarendon Press, 1946.

Crossman, Richard H. *The Charm of Politics*. New York: Harper, 1958.

Dawson, Raymond. *The Chinese Chameleon: An Analysis of European Conceptions of Chinese Civilization*. London: Oxford University Press, 1967.

Fisher, H. A. L. *Pages from the Past*. Oxford: Clarendon Press, 1939.

Frankel, Charles. *The Case for Modern Man*. New York: Harper, 1958.

Harcave, Sidney, ed. *Readings in Russian History*. Vol. 1. New York: Crowell, 1962. Essay by Dmitri Obolensky on Toynbee and Russian History.

Hocking, William E. *The Coming World Civilization*. New York: Harper, 1956. A globalist who quarrels with Toynbee for not recognizing that more things than religion survive in the intellectual tradition.

Kedourie, Elie. *The Chatham House Version and Other Middle-Eastern Studies*. New York: F. A. Praeger, 1970.

Manuel, Frank E. *Shapes of Philosophical History*. Stanford: Stanford University Press, 1965.

Mazlish, Bruce. *The Riddle of History: The Great Speculators from Vico to Freud*. New York: Harper and Row, 1966.

Namier, Sir Lewis. *Avenues of History*. London: Hamish Hamilton, 1952.

Popper, Karl. *The Open Society and Its Enemies*. Vol. 2. 4th ed. London: Routledge and Kegan Paul, 1962.

Wagar, W. Warren. *The City of Man*. Baltimore: Penguin Books, 1963.

Widgery, A. G. *Interpretations of History: Confucius to Toynbee*. London: Allen and Unwin, 1961.

ARTICLES

Africa, Thomas W. "The City of God Revisited: Toynbee's Reconsiderations." *Journal of the History of Ideas* 23 (1962), 282–92. Derisory; notes Toynbee's errors in ancient history.

———. "Phylarchus, Toynbee, and the Spartan Myth." *Journal of the History of Ideas* 21 (1960), 266–72.

Anderle, O. F. "A Plea for Theoretical History." *History and Theory* 4 (1964), 27–56, Pro-Toynbee. Anderle is trying to build a school of historical research on Toynbee's foundations, while correcting his errors.

———. "Toynbees Antwort an Seine Kritiker." *Historische Zeitschrift* 208 (1969), 81–97.

Argus, Jacob B. "Toynbee and Judaism." *Judaism* 4 (1955), 319–32.

Bartlett, R. M. "Toynbee on Korea." *Christian Century* 67 (1950), 946–47.

Bierstadt, Robert. "Toynbee and Sociology." *British Journal of Sociology* 10 (1959), 95–104. Sees Toynbee as a "speculative sociologist" and reflects on the connections between history and sociology.

Borkenau, Franz. "Toynbee's Judgment of the Jews." *Commentary* 9 (1955), 421–27.

Cameron, Meribeth. E. "A Bisection of Chinese History." *Pacific Historical Review* 8 (1939), 401–12.

———. "A Rehandling of Japanese History." *Far Eastern Quarterly* 1 (1942), 150–60.

Chase, Richard. "Toynbee: The Historian as Artist." *American Scholar* 16 (1947), 268–82.

Clarkson, Jesse D. "Toynbee on Slavic and Russian History." *Russian Review* 15 (1956), 165–72.

Dawson, Christopher. "Toynbee's Study of History: The Place of Civilization in History." *International Affairs* 31 (1955), 149–58; reprinted in his *The Dynamics of World History* (London: Sheed & Ward, 1957) and in Ashley Montagu. "My fundamental criticism

. . . is that it is too telescopic and that a true science of human cultures must be based on a more microscopic technique of anthropological and historical research." By a distinguished Roman Catholic student of history who regards it as a corrective to parochialism in time as well as space, and who thus views Toynbee with a basic sympathy.

Dray, William. "Toynbee's Search for Historical Laws." *History and Theory* 1 (1960), 32–54.

Feibleman, James. "Toynbee's Theory of History." *Southern Review* 5 (1960), 690–99.

Fogarty, Michael P. "The Rhythm of Change." *Review of Politics* 22 (1960), 451–65.

Fox, Edward T. "History and Mr. Toynbee." *Virginia Quarterly Review* 36 (1960), 458–61.

Gold, Milton. "Toynbee and the Turks in the Near and Middle East." *Journal of the Royal Society of Great Britain and Ireland*, 1961, pp. 77–99.

Griffith, Gwilym O. "Professor Toynbee, Mazzini, and the Future Faith." *Hibbert Journal* 54 (1956), 221–25.

Handlin, Oscar, "Toynbee: In the Dark Backward." *Partisan Review* 14 (1947), 371–79.

Harbison, E. Harris. "The Problem of the Christian Historian: A Critique of Arnold J. Toynbee." *Theology Today* 5 (1948), 388–405. Reprinted in his *Christianity and History*. Princeton: Princeton University Press, 1964. Sympathetic.

Hook, Sidney, "Mr. Toynbee's City of God." *Partisan Review* 15 (1948), 691–99.

Hudson, G. F. "Professor Toynbee Surrenders the West." *Commentary* 15 (1953), pp. 469–74. By an outstanding historian, of conservative, realist leanings.

Jerrold, Douglas. "Professor Toynbee, 'the West,' and the World." *Sewanee Review* 62 (1954), 56–83.

Kaufmann, Walter. "Toynbee: The Historian as False Prophet." *Commentary* 23 (1957), pp. 344–55. Kaufmann also has an article in Ashley Montagu.

Kempski, Jürgen von. "Stilisierte Geschichte." *Welt als Geschichte* 21 (1961), 131–57.

Lefebvre, Georges. "Compte rendu critique de Arnold J. Toynbee." *Revue historique* 201 (1949), 109–13. A distinguished French academician's verdict.

Letwin, Shirlye Robin. Review of *Surviving the Future*, by A. J. Toynbee. *Spectator*, September 4, 1971. Criticizes Toynbee's view of religion.

Millas Vallicross, José M. "Toynbee: Algunas objeciones a su obra historica." *Punta Europa* 3 (1958), 47–63. Notes some points from Spanish history, along with other objections.

Müller, Gert. "Toynbees Reconsiderations: Die Studie zur Weltgeschichte Neu Durchdacht." *Saeculum* 15 (1964), 311–26. Makes the valid point that Toynbee is disqualified by his moralism from coming to grips with the less spiritual side of human history.

Mumford, Lewis. "A Study of History." *Diogenes* 13 (1956), 11–28. See also Mumford's article in Ashley Montagu.

Pepin, Jean. "La religion d'un historien." *Mercure de France*, no. 1208 (1964), pp. 301–11.

Renou, Louis. "The Civilization of India according to Arnold Toynbee." *Diogenes* 13 (1956), 69–80.

Rotenstreich, Nathan. "The Revival of the Fossil Remnant." *Jewish Social Studies* 24 (1962), 131–43. Another round in the the war of Toynbee and Hebraism.

Roth, Eric. "A Theologian Looks at Professor Toynbee's Philosophy of History." *Hibbert Journal* 44 (1956), 213–20.

Sorokin, Pitirim. "Arnold J. Toynbee's Philosophy of History." *Journal of Modern History* 12 (1940), 374–87. Reprinted in Ashley Montagu.

Spate, O. H. K. *"Finis Coronat Opus?" Australian Outlook* 16 (1962), 84–89. See also Spate's essay on Toynbee as geographer, in Ashley Montagu.

Stammler, Heinrich, "Russia between Byzantium and Utopia." *Russian Review* 17 (1958), 94–103.

Stephanou, E. A. "Toynbee and Orthodox Christian Society." *Greek Orthodox Theological Review* 2 (1956), 27–40.

Talmon, J. L. "The Uniqueness and Universality of Jewish History." *Commentary* 24 (1957), 1–14. An exchange of views between Talmon and Toynbee may be found in *Congress Bi-Weekly* 34, November 6, 1967, 14–15.

Tawney, R. H. "Dr. Toynbee's Study of History." *International Affairs* 18 (1939), 798–806.

Thompson, Kenneth W. "Toynbee and International Politics." *Political Science Quarterly* 71 (1956), 365–86. Thompson's doctoral dissertation on this subject is on University Microfilm.

——. "Toynbee and World Politics," *Review of Politics* 18 (1956), 418–43.

Trevor-Roper, H. R. "Arnold Toynbee's Millennium." *Encounter* 45 (1957), 14–28. Reprinted in his *Historical Essays*. New York: Harper and Row, Torchbooks, 1966.

Vogt, Joseph. "Die Antike Kultur in Toynbee's Geschichtlehre." *Saeculum* 2 (1951), 557–74.

Walsh, W. H. "Toynbee Reconsidered." *Philosophy* 38 (1963), 71–78.

Watnick, Morris. "Toynbee's Nine Books of History against the Pagans." *Antioch Review* 7 (1947), 587–602.

Wendon, John. "Christianity, History, and Mr. Toynbee," *Journal of Religion* 36 (1956), 136–49.

Woodward, C. Vann, "Toynbee and Metahistory." *American Scholar*, 27 (1958), 384–92.

REVIEWS OF A *Study of History*

Barker, Sir Ernest. In *International Affairs* 31 (1955), 5–16. Reprinted in Ashley Montagu.

Beard, Charles A. In *American Historical Review* 45 (1940), 593–94.

Brinton, Crane. In *Yale Review* 29 (1940), 608–14.

Coulborn, Rushton. In *Cahiers d'Histoire Mondiale* 8 (1964), 15–53. An extensive review of *Reconsiderations*.

Hammond, J. L. In *Political Quarterly* 10 (1939), 545–61. For Toynbee's close friendship with J. L. and Barbara Hammond, the Socialist historians of the Industrial Revolution, see *Acquaintances*.

Hill, Christopher. In *Spectator*, May 12, 1961, pp. 685–86.

Hughes, H. Stuart. In *New York Herald-Tribune Books*, July 23, 1961, p. 4.

Kohn, Hans. In *Nation* 150 (1940), 256–57. Cf. Kohn's other articles on Toynbee in Ashley Montagu and Gargan.

Pares, Richard. In *English Historical Review* 71 (1956), 256–72.

Woolf, Leonard. In *New Statesman and Nation,* 18 (1939), 433.

GENERAL

Bagby, Philip. *Culture and History: Prolegomena to the Comparative Study of History.* London: Longmans, 1958. Finds only nine civilizations, and quarrels with Toynbee on classifications. Montgomery Belgion described the book as "childishly elementary." There exists a small library of similar exercises: cf. books by Carroll Quigley, Matthew Melko, and others.

Conkin, Paul K. and R. N. Stromberg, *The Heritage and Challenge of History.* New York: Dodd, Mead, 1971.

Donagan, Alan. "Historical Explanation: The Popper-Hempel Theory Reconsidered," *History and Theory* 4 (1965), 3–25.

Eliade, Mircea. *Cosmos and History.* New York: Harper and Row, 1959.

Fain, Haskell. *Between Philosophy and History: The Resurrection of Speculative Philosophy of History within the Analytical Tradition.* Madison: University of Wisconsin Press, 1970. Barely mentions Toynbee, but argues that "there is no reason why a speculative philosophy of history cannot have both good philosophy and good history," though heretofore such attempts have not succeeded because marked by inferior philosophy and inferior history.

Floud, Jean. *"The Evolution of Civilization: An Introduction to Historical Analysis,* by Carroll Quigley, and *On the Plurality of Civilizations,* by Feliks Koneczny," *History and Theory* 4 (1965), 271–75.

Geyl, Pieter. *Encounters in History.* New York: Meridian Books, 1961.

Hughes, H. Stuart. *Oswald Spengler: A Critical Estimate.* New York: Scribner's, 1952. On Toynbee's companion in crime; see especially pp. 138–42. On Spengler also, see J. H. Huizinga, "Two Wrestlers with an Angel." In *Dutch Civilization in the Seventeenth Century and other Essays,* New York: F. Ungar, 1968.

Leibel, Helen P. "The Historian and the Idea of World Civilization," *Dalhousie Review* 47 (1968), 455–66.

Lowith, Karl. *Meaning in History*. Chicago: University of Chicago Press, 1949.

McNeill, William H. *The Rise of the West: A History of the Human Community*. Chicago: University of Chicago Press, 1963.

Marcus, Tohn T. *Heaven, Hell and History*. New York and London: Macmillan, 1967.

Marrou, Henri I. *The Meaning of History* [De la connaissance historique]. Baltimore and Dublin: Halicon, 1966.

Ortega y Gasset. José, *Man and Crisis*. New York: Norton, 1958. Also London: George Allen and Unwin, 1959.

Popper, Karl. *The Poverty of Historicism*. Boston: Beacon Press, 1957.

Swabey, Marie C. *The Judgment of History*. New York: Philosophical Library, 1954.

Tinder, Glenn. "The Necessity of Historicism." *American Political Science Review* 55 (1961) 560–65.

Von Laue, Theodore H. "Is There a Crisis in the Writing of History?" *Bucknell Review* 14 (1966), 1–15.

Walsh, W. H. *Introduction to the Philosophy of History*. London: Hutchinson, 1951.

Westcott, Roger W. "The Enumeration of Civilizations." *History and Theory* 9 (1970), 59–85.

Wolf, Eric R. "Understanding Civilizations: A Review Article." *Comparative Studies in Society and History* 9 (1969), 446–65. The last two articles are both contributions to the literature studying how various historians have classified civilizations, and thus of central importance to students of Toynbee.

Index

Abraham, 31
Acton, Lord, 1, 16, 48
Aeschylus, 38
Africa, 95, 123, 131, 132
Africa, Thomas W., 141
Alexander the Great, 94
Altree, Wayne, 122
Anderle, O. F., 115, 141
Anthropology, 18, 57, 125
Aquinas, Thomas, 48–49
Argus, Jacob B., 141
Aristotle, 36, 48
Arnold, Matthew, 108, 120
Aron, Raymond, 57, 121, 127
Ashley Montagu, M. F., 115, 121
Augustine, Saint, xiii, 38, 77
Augustus, Emperor of Rome, 65

Bagby, Philip, 145
Bammate, N., 109, 123
Barker, Ernest, 2, 99, 113
Barraclough, Geoffrey, 49, 121, 122
Barrès, Maurice, 81
Barrett, David B., 132
Barth, Karl, 81, 82, 86, 130
Baumer, Franklin L., 65
Baynes, Norman R., 126, 127
Beard, Charles A., 46
Belgium, 5–6
Benda, Julien, 81

Bergson, Henri, 18, 22, 38, 54, 80, 118–19
Berlin, Isaiah, 125
Beus, J. G. de, 140
Bierstadt, Robert, 141
Borgese, G. A., 90
Borkenau, Franz, 141
Boulter, Veronica, 28
Bridges, Robert, 80
Brinton, Crane, 63, 144
Brooks, Van Wyck, 131
Browning, Robert, 38, 80, 103
Bryce, James, 1, 5, 8, 109
Buckle, Henry, xii, 53, 109
Buddhism, 25, 27, 67, 88, 96, 128, 130, 132
Bultmann, Rudolf, 130
Burckhardt, Jacob, xiii, 126
Butler, Samuel, 42
Butterfield, Herbert, 53
Byzantine (East Roman) Empire, 34, 61–63, 72, 126

Cameron, Meribeth, 122–23
Canning, George, 124
Carlyle, Thomas, 110
Carr, Edward H., 77
Céline, Louis-F., 81
Charlemagne, Emperor, 33, 35, 36, 61–62
Charles Martel, 33
Chase, Richard, 41
Chesterton, G. K., 86